CHRONICLES OF OLD CHICAGO

EXPLORING THE HISTORY AND LORE OF THE WINDY CITY

ADAM SELZER

Published in the United States by:
Museyon, Inc.
20 E. 46th St., Ste. 1400
New York, NY 10017

Museyon is a registered trademark.
Visit us online at www.museyon.com

ISBN 978-0-9846334-8-7

1459324

Printed in China

For generations now, Chicagoans have known that they can travel anywhere in the world, and everyone who hears where they come from will say, "Al Capone! Bang bang!"

Capone was only really in control of the city for about five years (and he spent most of that time out of town, in his Miami estate or in a Philadelphia prison cell). Still, his impact on the city, and the world's view of it, can't be denied. Think of Chicago, and you think of hot jazz music, men in overcoats running from the gangbusters, and dark city streets.

As images and reputations go, it could have been worse. It is certainly an image with more appeal than "Hog Butcher to the World," as Carl Sandburg once called the city. Going to see where the stockyards were just doesn't sound as exciting as going for a drink in an old speakeasy, which is remarkably easy to do in Chicago (go to Schaller's Pump, the city's oldest continually operating tavern, at 3714 South Halsted Street and ask them to show you the peephole). Gangsters and their speakeasies were everywhere in the 1920s, and some of the footprints and relics still survive.

But, of course, the city is more than just the city of gangsters. Chicago was a city designed to host world-class events, a great metropolis that rose from being "the Mudhole of the Prairie" (another old slogan that wouldn't exactly bring in the tourists today) to being one of the first cities with a million inhabitants in barely a single generation. Though the city might not have any 18th-century buildings (and just about everything from before 1871 was leveled in the Great Chicago Fire), it is still a city where it is easy to stand in the footprints of some of history's greats, from historical figures like Abraham Lincoln, Theodore Roosevelt, Jackie Robinson and Duke Ellington to more modern icons such as Oprah Winfrey, Michael Jordan and Roger Ebert, as you gaze up at an unparalleled skyline of skyscrapers stretching towards the sky, a jewel in the Midwest's crown.

And Chicago is far more than a city with a history—it is a city whose present makes it one of the most appealing cities in the world both to visit and to live in. One of very few cities in the United States where owning a car isn't really necessary, it is a city constantly on the move, with a new surprise around every corner.

And a story behind every street.

—Adam Selzer

Hog Butcher for the World,
Tool Maker, Stacker of Wheat,
Player with Railroads and the Nation's Freight Handler;
Stormy, husky, brawling,
City of the Big Shoulders:

from Carl Sandburg's poem, *Chicago,* 1914

CHRONICLES OF OLD CHICAGO

Sites that appear in the chapters

CHAPTER 1. ❶ The Site of Fort Dearborn
❷ The Site of The Battle of Fort Dearborn

CHAPTER 2. ❸ The Site of Sauganash

CHAPTER 3. ❹ Clark Street Bridge

CHAPTER 4. ❺ The Site of the Tremont House Hotel
❻ The Wigwam building

CHAPTER 5. ❼ The Stockyards Gate *(page 14)*

CHAPTER 6. ❽ The Site of Mrs. O'Leary's Home

CHAPTER 7. ❾ Lincoln Park *(page 14)*

CHAPTER 8. ❿ Dil Pickle Club
⓫ Statue of Captain Streeter

CHAPTER 9. ⓬ Hull House *(page 14)*

CHAPTER 10. ⓭ The Site of Everleigh Club *(page 14)*
⓮ The Site of the Coliseum

CHAPTER 11. ⓯ The Auditorium Theatre

CHAPTER 12. ⓰ Essanay Studios *(page 14)*
⓱ Selig Polyscope Building *(page 14)*

CHAPTER 13. ⓲ Comiskey Park (U.S. Cellular Field: *page 14)*

CHAPTER 14. ⓳ Old Courthouse Building

CHAPTER 15. ⓴ The Site of the Wind Blew Inn

CHAPTER 16. ㉑ The Site of the Saint Valentine's Day Massacre *(page 14)*

CHAPTER 17. ㉒ Resurrection Cemetery *(page 14)*

CHAPTER 18. ㉓ Billy Goat Tavern
㉔ Wrigley Field *(page 14)*

CHAPTER 19. ㉕ Drake Hotel

CHAPTER 20. ㉖ Bughouse Square (Washington Square)

CHAPTER 21. ㉗ Chess Records Studio (2120 S. Michigan Avenue) *(page 14)*

CHAPTER 22. ㉘ The Site of International Amphitheatre *(page 14)*

CHAPTER 23. ㉙ Harpo Studios *(page 14)*

CHAPTER 24. ㉚ Grant Park

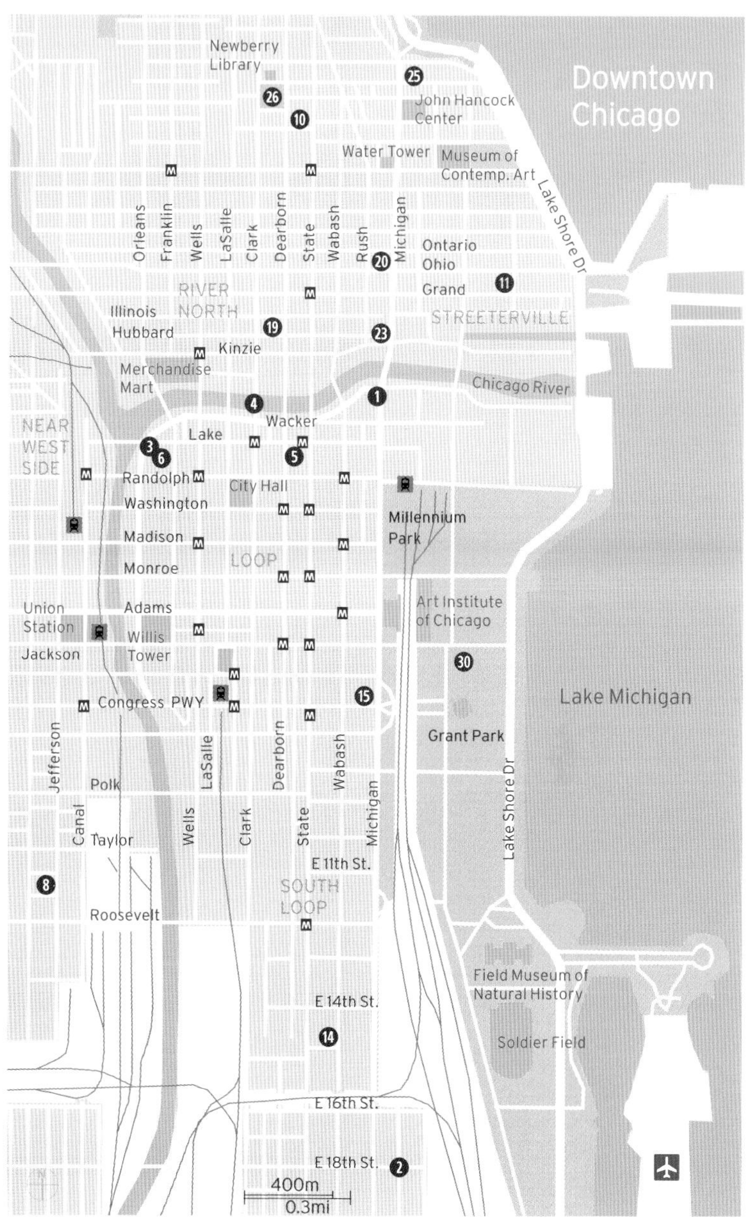
Downtown Chicago
Newberry Library
John Hancock Center
Water Tower
Museum of Contemp. Art
Lake Shore Dr
Orleans
Franklin
Wells
LaSalle
Clark
Dearborn
State
Wabash
Rush
Michigan
Ontario
Ohio
Grand
RIVER NORTH
Illinois
Hubbard
Kinzie
STREETERVILLE
Merchandise Mart
Chicago River
Wacker
NEAR WEST SIDE
Lake
Randolph
City Hall
Washington
Millennium Park
Madison
Monroe
LOOP
Union Station
Adams
Art Institute of Chicago
Willis Tower
Jackson
Congress PWY
Lake Michigan
Grant Park
Jefferson
Polk
Canal
Taylor
E 11th St.
SOUTH LOOP
Roosevelt
Field Museum of Natural History
E 14th St.
Soldier Field
E 16th St.
E 18th St.
400m
0.3mi

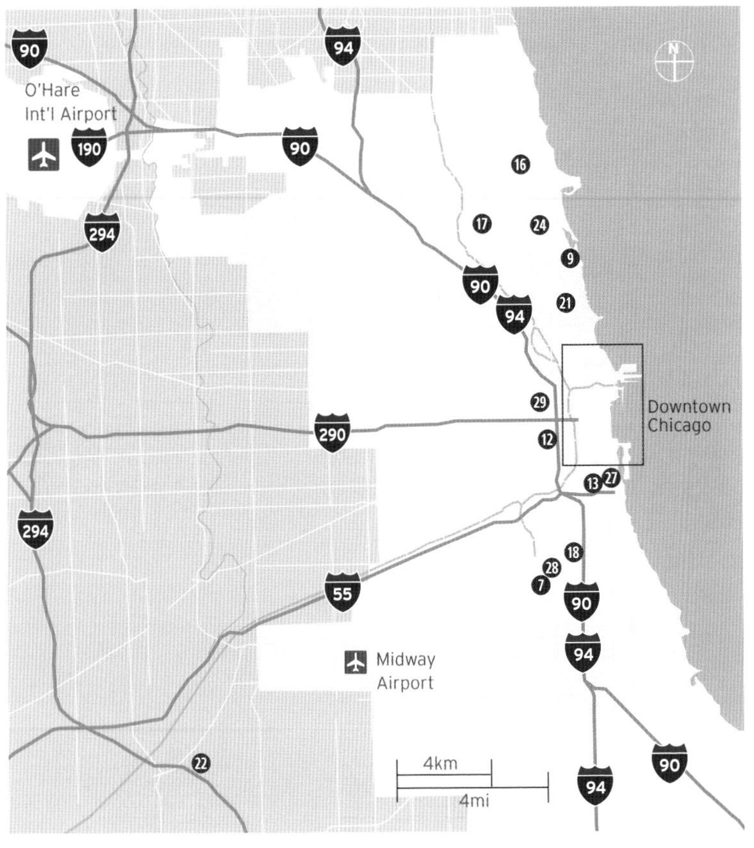
90
94
O'Hare
Int'l Airport
190
90
16
294
17
24
9
90
21
94
29
Downtown
Chicago
290
12
13
27
294
18
28
7
55
90
94
Midway
Airport
22
4km
4mi
94
90

- 7 The Stockyards Gate
- 9 Lincoln Park
- 12 Hull House
- 13 The Site of Everleigh Club
- 16 Essanay Studios
- 17 Selig Polyscope Building
- 18 Comiskey Park (U.S. Cellular Field)
- 21 The Site of the Saint Valentine's Day Massacre
- 22 Resurrection Cemetery
- 24 Wrigley Field
- 27 Chess Records Studio (2120 South Michigan Avenue)
- 28 International Amphitheatre
- 29 Harpo Studios

CHAPTER 1.

THE BATTLE OF FORT DEARBORN: HOW THE WORLD FIRST HEARD OF THIS PLACE CALLED CHEEKAGEAUXS

1812

In 1816, when soldiers came to the area known as "Chicageaux" to build a new Fort Dearborn—named for Henry Dearborn, who was secretary of war from 1801-09—they were greeted with an unpleasant sight: the bones of the soldiers who had founded the old fort, which had been bleaching in the sun since the day the first fort was burned to the ground.

At the time of the War of 1812, the space that would one day be Chicago was hardly a major outpost; it was just a place where the river met Lake Michigan, a region that the local Potawatomi Indians called "Eschecagou" (or any of a dozen other spellings), which referred to the foul smell of wild onions and garlic that hovered over the area. There was a fort there, but only a small and poorly armed one that stood on the edge of what was then a nearly unimaginable wilderness—even a generation later, you could still go hunting for big game just as close to the city as the present site of Halsted Street, just blocks west of the Loop, the main downtown area. Besides a few settlers who lived near the mouth of the river, and many Potawatomi Indians who lived in the

 Defense, Henry Hering, 1928. The Battle of Fort Dearborn is commemorated on the site of Fort Dearborn at the tender's house of the Michigan Avenue Bridge

DEFENSE!

Fort Dearborn over Kinzie mansion and Jean Baptiste Point du Sable

vicinity, the soldiers of the fort and their families—just over a hundred people—were among America's last lines of defense of the frontier.

The first non-native to settle in the area was Jean Baptiste Point du Sable, about whom fairly little is known. In the late 1770s he was arrested on suspicion of sympathizing with the colonists in the Revolutionary War (which was illegal when the colonies were still colonies), but it is unclear what brought him to Chicago, where he settled around the 1780s. Some suggest that he was a Caribbean pirate on the run from the law. That may seem far-fetched, but it is probably as good an explanation as any for why he, or anyone else, would have settled in what was then such a desolate place.

Most stories about his early life, parentage, and origins are guesswork at best, and impossible to authenticate today, though it's generally agreed that he was at least part African-American. People who knew him described him as handsome and well-educated. Traders passing through the area where he lived were known to buy goods from him; he had his own farm, flour mill, dairy, two barns, a chicken coop and a smoke house. The cabin he shared with his Potawatomi wife was spacious, comfortably appointed, and well decorated. He moved on from the area in 1800, allegedly because the local tribes wouldn't make him chief, probably never dreaming that a monument on the site of his cabin would one day designate him as the "founder of Chicago." After all, there was no Chicago there yet!

Point du Sable sold his house to one Jean La Lime, a trader, who immediately became a fierce rival of the *other* local trader, John Kinzie (whose social-climbing daughter-in-law would work hard to make future generations refer to *him* as the founder of the city). In those days, the market for a trading post was minimal; few trappers came through the area, so competition for the two men got fierce. Eventually, the rivalry became deadly when Kinzie killed La Lime in 1812.

Now, what actually happened between the two men is not exactly known. The official story was that La Lime attacked Kinzie, shooting him in the shoulder, and Kinzie was acting in self-defense when he stabbed La Lime to death. Many, however, doubt the story—few men who have been shot in the shoulder are in good enough shape to stab a man to death in the moments after the shooting. Many modern historians think that the fight between the two was really just a drunken brawl between a couple of prairie ruffians, and speculate the soldiers at the fort had been annoyed with La Lime, who perhaps was threatening to expose corruption within the fort.

Old Fort Dearborn erected in 1803, A.T. Andreas, *History of Chicago*. Fort Dearborn was constructed by troops under Captain John Whistler and named in honor of Henry Dearborn, then United States Secretary of War

Life at the fort went on like this, with minor dramas and fights, until the War of 1812, when tensions between early Americans and the British turned into a second war against the two nations. When word came that the British soldiers (whose support of Native American tribes against American expansion was one of the sore points that sparked the war) were marching on Fort Dearborn, orders came in to evacuate—the little fort had nowhere near the supplies to fight back the British Army. Arrangements were made for the settlers and their families to set out on foot for Fort Wayne, but they never made it more than a couple of miles from the city before being attacked by the Potawatomi.

Determining the true history of what happened at The Battle of Fort Dearborn—otherwise known as the Fort Dearborn Massacre—has frustrated historians; several first- and second-hand accounts were written of the horrific fight, but no one seemed to be able to retell the story without trying to make themselves look like a hero. From comparing different accounts, though, we can put some of the basics together.

Having received orders to evacuate the fort before the British Army could arrive, the captain of the fort, Nathan Heald, met with the Potawatomi and offered them a deal: if they would accompany the soldiers and their families to Fort Wayne, the settlers would give them all their guns, all their ammunition, and all of their whiskey.

The Potawatomi agreed to the deal, but the other officers in the fort thought that Heald had lost his mind—tensions between the settlers and the tribe had been running high, and he had just offered potentially hostile people guns, ammunition, and liquor. Heald agreed that it had been a bad idea, and the weapons were thrown down a well. The whiskey was poured into the river in such quantities that people noted that the drinking water tasted of "strong grog" the next day.

Perhaps the Potawatomi saw the settlers destroying the goods they had promised them and decided that the passage to Fort Wayne would not be a safe one. Or, they may have decided that before.

Shortly before the group set off, Captain William Wells had arrived.

The Fort Dearborn Massacre, Samuel Page; and William Wells, son-in-law of Miami Chief Little Turtle

Raised by the Miami Tribe himself, Wells was something of a legend among the frontiersmen; he was said to speak several Native American languages. His niece, Rebecca, was married to Captain Nathan Heald, and he, along with a small band of Miami warriors, had come to help the settlers move.

In any case, when the settlers set off for Fort Wayne accompanied by a band of Potawatomi warriors, they only got a mile south—down to the present day site of 18th Street and Prairie Avenue—before the warriors turned on the settlers and attacked them.

The battle only lasted about fifteen minutes—the settlers and the Miami were greatly outnumbered by the Potawatomi.

Margaret Helm, the wife of a fort lieutenant, found Dr. Van Voorhees, the fort surgeon, lying wounded in the sand, and as the battle raged on, he suggested to her that they surrender and beg for their lives.

"Dr. Voorhees," said Mrs. Helm, "do not let us waste the moments that yet remain to us in such vain hopes. Our fate is inevitable. In a few moments we must appear before the bar of God. Let us make what preparation is yet in our power."

"Oh, I cannot die!" shouted Voorhees. "I am not fit to die if I had but a

Fort Dearborn Massacre Monument by Carl Rohl-Smith, 1893. Chief Black Partridge intervenes to save the life of Margaret Helm

short time to prepare. Death is awful!"

Helm pointed out Ensign George Ronan, who was fighting with his last breath, though he was mortally wounded. "Look at that man," she said. "At least he dies like a soldier!"

"Yes," said the doctor, "but he has no terrors of the future. He is an atheist!"

Just at that moment, a warrior raised his tomahawk over Mrs. Helm, and she rolled away just in time for it to hit her shoulder instead of her head. The chief of the Potawatomi warriors, Black Partridge, grabbed her and took her to the safety of the nearby lake.

Or, anyway, that was the way Mrs. Helm told the story. Whether it was real or strictly fiction on her part is anyone's guess (though Dr. Voorhees did, in fact, die in the battle).

When she was led to safety, Helm claimed to see another warrior holding a scalp, which she recognized as that of Captain William Wells. He had been shot in the back and killed in the battle; several accounts say that his heart was cut out and eaten by other warriors as a tribute to his courage.

The 500 warriors greatly outnumbered the hundred-odd settlers and soldiers. Within only 15 minutes, around 50 of the soldiers and settlers were killed, and the survivors were captured and sold as slaves to the British (who, to their credit, promptly let them go). The fort was burned to the ground, and the bodies of several settlers were left to rot on the dunes.

Word of the battle was the first many people would hear of the little village called Chicago.

The borders of the Fort are marked with plaques on the ground near the corner of Wacker Drive and Michigan Avenue, right at the foot of what is now the Magnificent Mile. It's almost impossible to imagine that only two centuries ago it was the edge of the frontier.

THE FLAG OF CHICAGO

The flag of the city of Chicago features four stars, each representing a major event in the city's history. The first star is for the Battle of Fort Dearborn. The second is for the Great Chicago Fire of 1871, and third and fourth stars are for the World's Fairs hosted in 1893 and 1933.

CHAPTER 2.

CHICAGO IS BORN: FROM MUDHOLE TO METROPOLIS

1837

People joking about Chicago elections often say that the slogan is to "Vote Early, Vote Often." According to legend, that practice goes all the way back to the founding of the city. When the settlers voted to incorporate as a city in 1837, 150 votes were needed, but only 140 people showed up to vote. To get to the "magic number," ten of the men simply voted twice.

This would have been in the 1830s, when Chicago was still not even big enough to be called "the mudhole of the prairie." By then, it had been inhabited by settlers for more than a quarter of a century, but growth was coming in fits and starts. It was hard to imagine back then just how rapidly the city would soon grow; it took human civilization thousands of years to produce a city with a million residents, and Chicago went from nearly zero to more than a million in just over half a century.

By 1833, the little village had reached a population of around 200 settlers and traders, none of whom imagined that the little village they had settled in would be a sprawling metropolis within their lifetimes,

 Chicago in 1820, Chicago Lithographing Co., c. 1867 (top) and *Chicago, As It Was*, between 1856 and 1907

though many land speculators moved in with a hunch that the tracts of land near the river and lake would one day be far more valuable. In that year, the Treaty of Chicago moved the native tribes to a new five-million acre reservation west of the Mississippi, and travelers described the settlement as an important trading center where locals did business with settlers who were heading farther west. But, though it was becoming an important town, in its way, it was still not exactly a pretty one—it was still little more than a conglomeration of shacks set up in the mud at the mouth of the river. One traveler described "a chaos of mud, rubbish and confusion. Frame and clapboard houses were springing up daily under the active axes and hammers of the speculators, and piles of lumber announced the preparation for yet other edifices of an equally light character."

By this time, the city had several stores, a couple of doctors, five or six hotel keepers, and a steady stream of transient residents, some of whom impressed witnesses as "sharpers'" (con men) "of every degree." Most grocery stores really only sold whiskey. At least one hotel, though, the Sauganash, was known as fairly plush by the standards of the day. It stood at the present site of Wacker and Lake Street, and the five-block journey to the main fort was usually made by river, as the roads were so muddy that they were impossible to walk through.

It's a wonder, really, that there was anyone left in town by then, as 1831 was described as "the winter of deep snow," when snow was four feet deep and the temperature hovered at 15 below for three weeks. Freezing to death was one of the most common causes of death, if not the

Last Council of the Potawatomies. Lawrence Carmichael Earle, 1833, originally painted for the Banking Room of the Central Trust Company of Illinois in Chicago

The Sauganash Tavern hosted the city's first elections; and William B. Ogden, George Peter Alexander Healy, 1855

most common of all, and it's remarkable that any survived it at all. The cold served at least one useful purpose, though; when ice formed on the lake, the businesses in town would close for a day and all of the wolves in the woods would be driven out to the ice to be shot. This was one of the most festive days of the year.

By 1831, Chicago was already the county seat of Cook County, but was not yet officially a town at all. In that year, a law was passed saying that an area could become a town if the population reached 150, and two years later it met the requirement.

The legend that only 140 showed up to vote, prompting 10 to vote twice, seems to be just that—a legend. The rule was that you needed 150 people, not 150 votes. On August 3rd, Justice of the Peace Ralph E. Hickok presided over a meeting of the citizens of Chicago at the Sauganash Tavern about incorporating, and a vote was held among those present. Twelve men voted to incorporate, and only Hickok himself voted against it. The resolution to incorporate as a town was adopted. Four years later, it was incorporated as a full-fledged city. William Ogden was elected mayor, beating out John Kinzie's son for the title.

By 1840, the population of Chicago had reached 4,000. The construction of the Illinois-Michigan canal brought in scores of men looking for

Raising of a block of brick buildings on Lake Street, Chicago, in 1857

work, and made the area economically viable. Speculators bought up broad parcels of land in something of a frenzy.

John Wentworth, an early mayor, later noted that most new settlements can be pointed out by "a particular class," such as the Puritans in New England or the Creoles of New Orleans. But Chicago had no such class—it was a broad mix of races, religions, classes and creeds. In many ways it was the most American of cities.

By the time of the World's Fair in 1893, when Chicago truly announced itself to the world as a major city, there were still people alive in town who remembered the city as it had been when they were children: simply a small collection of wooden houses on the muddy prairie. None could have dreamed that their little town would become the greatest metropolis of the Midwest.

STREET NAMES

Many of the streets in the Loop today have the same names they had in 1833. Clark Street was named after George Clark, the "conqueror of the Illinois Country." LaSalle was named for the explorer, Franklin for Ben Franklin, and Fulton for the inventor of the steamship. Names like "State" and "Lake" were simply generic street names

HARPER THE DRUNK

By then, the town had its own town crier, who would announce land sales and put on musical entertainments at night. The crier was also the buyer in what some have described as the city's only slave auction—a particularly odd one, in that the buyer was black and the "slave" was white. Slavery was never illegal in Illinois, but in the early 1830s, prisoners from the jail who couldn't pay for their board could be sold into indentured servitude until the debt was paid off. Such was the case for poor "Harper the Drunk," who seems to have been put on sale mainly to humiliate him into reforming. George White, the town crier, bought him for a quarter, but Harper ran off before doing any work for him.

CHAPTER 3.

THE LAGER BEER RIOTS: CHICAGO GETS WHAT IT DESERVES FOR ELECTING A MAYOR FROM THE "KNOW NOTHING" PARTY

1855

Chicago has long been known for the battles fought between forces of the law and people who just wanted to have a drink. The battle between bootleggers and gangbusters in the 1920s is a part of what defined the modern era's perception of the city.

But few realize that the city's first battle for legal drinking came decades before, in 1855.

Chicago always had a flair for electing strange mayors—people with names like Long John and Big Bill. Elected in 1915, William Hale Thompson, known as Big Bill, displayed antics and buffoonery, in particular, such as hosting debates with rodents standing in for his opponents, which earned him a place in Chicago history, if not exactly a place of honor.

But few remember that Chicago once elected a member of the Know Nothing Party as the mayor.

Uncle Sam's youngest son, Citizen Know Nothing, c. 1854. This bust portrait of the young man represents the nativist ideal of the Know Nothing Party

UNCLE SAM'S YOUNGEST SON
CITIZEN
KNOW NOTHING.
91.
Williams, Stevens, Williams & Co. 353 Broadway, N.Y.

The mid-1800s were an age of odd political parties. Besides the once-powerful Whig Party (which mainly existed to oppose the Democrats by then), there was the Free Silver party, the Anti-Mason party, and countless others. Perhaps the most colorfully-named of them all was the Know Nothing Party, so called because of its renowned secrecy. When asked what their platform was, exactly, members were supposed to say "I know nothing." The mid 1800s were such a volatile time, politically, that even a party that wouldn't reveal its platform was a viable and electable party. Most people just knew the basics: that the Know-Nothings were anti-immigrant and anti-Catholic. Abraham Lincoln detested them; he wrote to a friend that, "As a nation, we began by declaring that '*all men are created equal*.' We now practically read it, "*all men are created equal except negroes*." When the Know-nothings get control, it will read, '*all men are created equal except negroes and foreigners and Catholics*.' When it comes to this, I shall prefer emigrating to some country where they make no pretense of loving liberty—to Russia, for instance, where despotism can be taken pure, and without the base alloy of hypocrisy."

Levi Boone, a party member, was elected mayor of Chicago in 1855, defeating incumbent Isaac Milliken, shortly before Lincoln wrote his outraged letter. As mayor, he promptly enacted policies in line with the Know Nothing platform: anti-alcohol and anti-immigrant. He tripled the number of police on the streets (for which he deserves some credit); however, he barred immigrants from holding city jobs and raised the cost of liquor licensing fees from $50 to $300, which was considered a blow to immigrants because many tavern owners at the time were immigrants.

Indeed, many of the saloon keepers who needed such a license in the first place were poor immigrants from Germany and Ireland—the people that the Know Nothings hated most of all—and many of the tavern-owners felt that raising the license fee was a targeted attack on them (which, no doubt, it was). This angered them enough, but the last straw was when Boone pushed through an ordinance closing all the beer gardens on Sundays. Drinking was a long-established part of Sunday relaxation for many immigrants (it was the only day they got off from work) and the loss of a full day's business hit saloon keepers hard.

Scene of a lager beer tavern and Levi Boone, 14th Mayor of Chicago (1855-1856)

Most saloon keepers seem to have reacted to the law the same way people a few generations later would react to Prohibition—by ignoring the rules completely. Early on, a number of saloon keepers were arrested for violating the ordinance.

On April 21, 1855, only weeks after Boone took office, a handful of protesters—perhaps as many as 300 saloon keepers—clashed with the police outside of the courthouse that stood on Clark and Washington streets, eventually being pushed back a block to Clark and Randolph. "Here," the *Tribune* later remembered, "the first violence took place. An attempt to make an arrest was resisted by the mob, and for half an hour the knock-downs, beating and fighting were lively, but the mob gave way, and retreated to the North Side for 'reinforcements.'"

Gather for reinforcements they did, and as they congregated in their neighborhoods just north of the river, the downtown citizens were abuzz with rumors of what was happening for several hours. Meanwhile, Mayor Boone sent for reinforcements of his own. There were a few false alarms, but then word went out that "the North Side is coming!"

In late afternoon, the mob assembled to the beat of a fife and drum on the Clark Street Bridge, marching in tight military formation and armed with whatever arms they could cobble together. They marched right across the bridge and fired a volley at the courthouse as spectators watched from the rooftops and balconies of the buildings nearby.

Clark Street Bridge, c. 1865-1915

They didn't have time to reload before they were fired upon by the police. Unable to regroup for a big fight, the mob ran back to the Clark Street Bridge.

The bridge, in those days, was a swing bridge—the kind that could swivel around to allow ships to pass through. The mayor ordered the bridge open, leaving the protesters stranded in the middle of the river.

Both sides, though, were armed, and the police began to fire on the protesters. The protesters fired back, costing one police officer his leg, and the bridge was put back in place to allow protesters to retreat. About 60 men were arrested, though few were ever brought to trial, and even fewer were ever found guilty of anything.

Whether anyone was killed in the riot remains something of an open question today—rumors flew through the city that several men had died, and the fact that cannons had been pointed at the bridge didn't do much to dispel these rumors. However, it seems that the casualties were very low. Some say that one single protester was killed, and some say that none were killed at all.

Still, for several days, the "North Side" was viewed as an "insurrectionary district," and several hundred ordinary citizens were deputized as special police officers in case of another flare-up, which was rumored to be brewing at any time. Brass guns were mounted at every corner of Court House Square, and the area around it was placed under martial law for a few days.

But with or without casualties, the fact that the riot had happened on Mayor Boone's watch escaped no one, and he was soundly voted out of office the next year. In the year or two that followed, internal debates over the all-encompassing question of slavery would tear the Know Nothing Party apart, just as they would soon nearly tear the country itself apart, as well.

CHILDREN AND BOOZE

Some in Chicago have always opposed any limits to drinking well into the late 19th century; saloon keepers were known to protest that laws banning them from selling whiskey to children were unconstitutional. Children were still allowed to go "can rushing"—buying booze from saloons for their parents—until 1904.

CHAPTER 4.

ABRAHAM LINCOLN COMES TO CHICAGO: CHICAGO WAS ALMOST A SECOND HOME TO THE SIXTEENTH PRESIDENT

1858-60

The cupola that crowned Judge Ebenzer Peck's north side mansion offered clear views of Lake Michigan to the east, and of City Cemetery to the south. In 1860, when President-elect Abraham Lincoln visited the house, it is easy to picture him standing in the cupola, looking out at the cemetery (which would soon become the park that bears his name) and contemplating the Civil War that was looming before him and the nation. A rift between northern and southern states had been obvious for years, owing largely to the fact that slavery was still legal in the southern states, and the southern states had threatened to secede from the Union and form a country of their own. It had been an idle threat before, but when Lincoln was elected with barely a single southern vote, many states announced their intention to secede from the Union. A war between the states was about to begin, and soon the cemetery that Lincoln would have beheld from that cupola would be filled with thousands of soldier's graves.

Lincoln never lived in Chicago, but Chicagoans considered him one of their own. In 1858, he gave a version of his famous "House Divided"

 Lincoln's address at the dedication of the Gettysburg National Cemetery, November 19, 1863

speech from the balcony of the Tremont House Hotel on Dearborn (just south of Lake Street, where the parking garage is now). "The audience to hear Honorable Abraham Lincoln on Saturday Evening was, in point of numbers, about three-fourths as large as that of the previous evening, when Douglas held forth," wrote the *Tribune.* "And in point of enthusiasm, about four times as great. The crowd extended from the corner of Lake and Dearborn Streets (to) the whole length of the Tremont House, and, as on the evening previous, the balconies, windows and roofs of adjoining buildings were filled with attentive spectators—ladies and gentlemen." The paper estimated the crowd at roughly 9,000.

Tremont House Hotel, Louis Kurz, 1866

Lincoln, who was hoping to become senator, was making speeches in support of the newly formed Republican Party, which had risen from the ashes of Lincoln's old party, the Whigs. Democrat Stephen Douglas was the senator at the time, but if Republicans could take control of the state legislature, Lincoln would be named as the senator (which is how senate elections worked in those days; direct election of senators is relatively new). In Lincoln's Chicago speech, he stood on the balcony and repeated one of the best lines from his recent Springfield speech: "A house divided against itself cannot stand. I believe this government cannot endure permanently half slave and half free." Anti-Lincoln agitators today insist that Lincoln never argued for ending slavery, only for stopping the spread of it, but in the speech he said that he hoped "the opponents of slavery will arrest the spread of it and place it where the public mind shall rest in the belief that it is in the course of ultimate extinction."

Still, though, in his Chicago speech, he made great pains to say that he didn't think the north had any right to outlaw slavery in places where it was already on the books; he merely hoped that it would die out on its own if it wasn't allowed to spread, and he assumed that it would take decades.

But taking this fairly moderate position was exactly the course that was needed in those days, and it put Lincoln in a position to bring about slavery's end far sooner than he had predicted. The Republicans failed to win enough seats to send Lincoln to the Senate in 1858, so he spent 1859 traveling the country, making variations on the same speech and making enough of a name for himself that in 1860, when it came time to nominate candidates for president to succeed James Buchanan, his name was among those mentioned. Just being on the long list of possible candidates was something of a coup in itself for a man whose major political experience up to that point was a short, relatively undistinguished stint in the House of Representatives as a member of a party that no longer existed.

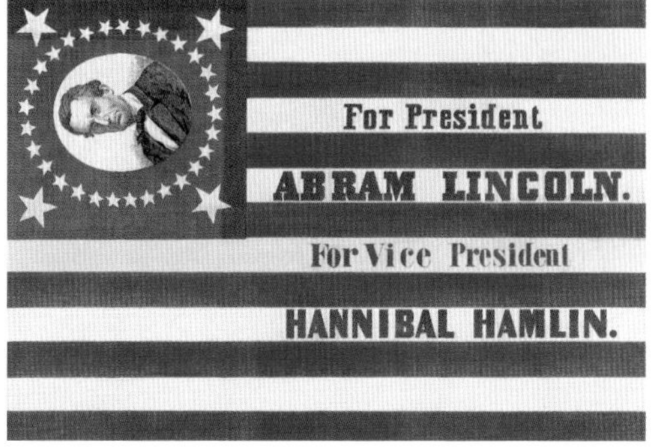

An 1850 campaign banner with Lincoln's first name misspelled

Throughout the 1850s, Chicago had been a home-away-from-home for the future president; as a traveling lawyer, he made regular appearances at the U.S. Circuit Court in Chicago in July and December. He had first come to town for a political convention in 1847, and those who met him were impressed mainly by how strangely he looked and dressed. Though not yet 40 years old at the time, people called him "Old Abe," and one contemporary, a lawyer named Leonard Swett, said that "No one who saw him can forget his personal appearance at that time. Tall, angular, and awkward, he had on a short-waisted, thin swallow-tail coat, a short vest of the same material, thin pantaloons, scarcely coming to his ankles, a straw hat and a pair of brogans with woolen socks." It is difficult to imagine Lincoln in any hat other than a stovepipe today without chuckling.

But as strange as he looked (and, by most accounts, sounded, as his reedy tenor voice occasionally raised to falsetto), his powers as a speaker impressed everyone who met him, and besides his many trips to town to argue legal cases, he appeared regularly in the city as a political speaker, usually staying at the Tremont House, which was ground zero for visiting politicians at the time. After the Lincoln-Douglas debates in 1858, political speechmaking became more or less Lincoln's full-time job. He came to town several times in 1859, both as a politician and as a lawyer, often meeting with Mayor John Wentworth, with whom he had served in Congress.

In May of 1860, the Republican National Convention was held in Chicago at the Republican Wigwam building, a stadium erected at what is now the corner of Wacker and Lake. At the time, the "safe money" was on New York Senator William Seward, a distinguished politician in his own right. Nearly everyone assumed that he would be nominated; his hometown had already hired a band to play when the announcement was made.

But conventions then were much different than they are today. It has now been many years since the identity of a nominee wasn't a foregone conclusion at a convention, and the nomination is generally made after a single ballot. Years ago, this wasn't the case; well into the 20th century, conventions that required dozens of ballots to determine a nominee were still fairly common. Most who were putting money on the nomination would have bet on Seward, but when the votes were counted after the first ballot, Seward hadn't secured enough votes to be nominated.

Seward was in first place, but a strong second-place showing was made by Lincoln. Lincoln was not in attendance at the time (it was then considered improper for nominees to appear at the convention), but strong forces were working on his behalf. While Seward's still-confident supporters left the Wigwam for a parade, Mayor John Wentworth filled

The Wigwam, the building constructed for the 1860 Republican Convention in Chicago, and a portrait of Lincoln by an Illinois photographer Alexander Hesler in early June 1860

their places in with Lincoln supporters, and their cheers made delegates who hadn't seriously considered Lincoln as a candidate reconsider him. The fact that he had been endorsed for president by the local papers didn't hurt, either.

Lincoln was, after all, a moderate voice, and Seward was so identified with the radical wing of the party that delegates feared that he wouldn't have the crossover appeal necessary to get elected, even with the Democratic Party (which nominated Douglas) in total disarray. And as fears that Seward couldn't win the general election mounted, Lincoln's men were working hard to convince delegates to make Lincoln their second choice.

On the second ballot, Lincoln and Seward were nearly tied, and on the third ballot, Lincoln was nominated. Some believe that it would not have been possible to nominate him in any other city, and that the nomination of Lincoln was the great gift to the world that only Chicago could have provided. Chicago celebrated the nomination in grand style: A hundred guns were fired from the roof of the Tremont House, and the crowds took to the streets, carrying aloft a couple of the rails reputed to be rails split by Lincoln himself back in his early days, when he famously worked as a rail splitter.

After winning the election Lincoln returned to Chicago once more, where he met with Hannibal Hamlin, the vice president-elect, for the first time at the Tremont House. Lincoln took Hamlin on a short tour of the city, including a trip to the Wigwam where they had been nominated, as well as all of the major government buildings. The next morning, a public reception was held at the Tremont House, where a crowd of thousands braved the cold, snowy weather to shake the president and vice president-elect's hands. Hamlin was amazed by the magnificent buildings ("some of them (are) palaces," he wrote to his wife), and with the fact that Chicago had grown from nearly nothing to a town of more than 100,000 people in only 25 years. Shortly thereafter, they met at Ebenezer Peck's north side mansion to determine who would form Lincoln's cabinet.

Despite the celebration in Chicago, Lincoln and Hamlin could not have failed to realize that their term in the White House would not be an easy one. By the time they were inaugurated, seven states had announced their intention to secede from the Union. Though some today claim that slavery was a very small part of their reasons for doing so, states

Arch at Twelfth Street, Chicago, with President Abraham Lincoln's hearse and a procession of women, S.M. Fassett, 1865

that issued "articles of secession" made it abundantly clear that their primary purpose was to preserve the "peculiar institution." Lincoln's first term and re-election campaign were consumed by the bloody Civil War that resulted.

John Wilkes Booth, between 1861 and 1865

Lincoln never returned to Chicago alive, but after his assassination by actor John Wilkes Booth in 1865, which occurred just as the war was finally winding to a close, his body was taken on tour around the country so that mourners in every major city would have a chance to pay their last respects. In Chicago, the president's body was lain in state in the Old Courthouse at Clark and Washington, where City Hall now stands. Prior to laying in state, his funeral procession traveled up Michigan Avenue before a crowd of thousands. Chicago had been the fallen president's home away from home in life, and he had personally been able to see it rise from the small jumble of a town that it was in the 1840s to its early days as a major metropolis.

Little of the Chicago he knew is still standing today. The Republican Wigwam, the Tremont House, and most of the rest of the town was destroyed in the Great Chicago Fire of 1871. However, the chapel of Saint James Church, at Huron and Wabash, survives, and a tablet commemorates the day when President-elect Lincoln attended services there. A few blocks away on Chicago Avenue stands the Abraham Lincoln Book Shop, a headquarters for collectors and scholars of Lincoln memorabilia. Current items for sale include a letter written and signed by Lincoln on the same day he signed the preliminary Emancipation Proclamation, the last portrait of Lincoln drawn "from the flesh" (a drawing of him in his coffin) and several relics from the 1860 presidential campaign.

JOHN WILKES BOOTH PLAYS SHAKESPEARE

John Wilkes Booth, Lincoln's assassin, spent a few weeks in 1862 starring in a variety of Shakespeare plays at the old McVicker's Theatre on Madison Street. A disturbing number of the roles called for monologues in which he plotted assassinations. Critics generally considered his brother, Edwin, to be the superior actor, but the *Tribune* thought that John Wilkes' erratic interpretations of Shakespeare's great roles were ingenious.

LINCOLN'S BURIAL PLACE

Chicago nearly became Lincoln's burial place. When Springfield wanted to bury him in the Town Square, not at Oak Ridge Cemetery, as his widow requested, she threatened to bury him in Chicago. Exactly where he would be interred was an open question up until the funeral train arrived in Springfield.

Mary Lincoln moved to Chicago after she left Washington; she lived in the west Loop area on Washington Boulevard; her son Tad walked through nearby Union Square Park on the way to his school, where he helped create what is thought to be the first grade-school newspaper.

Abraham Lincoln, candidate for U.S. president, three-quarter length portrait, before delivering his Cooper Union address in New York City, 1860

CHAPTER 5.

THE STOCKYARDS THAT MADE CHICAGO: HOW CHICAGO GOT THE NAME "THE HOG BUTCHER FOR THE WORLD"

1864-1971

The Chicago Stockyards changed the world. They certainly changed Chicago. The rise of railroads, and the invention of refrigerated train cars, made it possible for meat to be processed in one large, central location and then shipped all over the country. Chicago, situated as it was in the center of the United States and adjacent to many railroads, became the perfect place to centralize the packing companies. A group of nine railroad companies went in together in 1864 to purchase 320 acres of swampland on the southwest side of the city, and meatpackers such as Armour, Swift, and other giants of the day, set up stockyards in the grounds. By 1870, the companies at the Union Stockyards were processing around two million animals per year, and that number would more than quadruple over the next 20 years. At of the turn of the 20th century, nearly half a billion heads of livestock had been butchered in the stockyards.

The stockyards became something of a city in their own right, with its own fire department, police force, chapel, inn, and an exposition building. Some of the meatpacking companies took their places among

 In the heart of the Great Union Stockyards, c. 1909

ARM
NORTH AMERICAN PROVISION CO.

The Great Union Stockyards of Chicago, c. 1878

the largest and most successful organizations that the world had ever known.

The stockyard owners were famous for their resourcefulness, and were always looking for new ways to make money from the byproducts of the animals. Parts that weren't made into meat could be used for glues, leather, shoe polish, fertilizer and countless other projects. A common joke said that the companies in the stockyards used "everything but the squeal."

These stockyards were, in many ways, an immense boon for Chicago, attracting thousands of migrant workers and providing steady employment for countless people. The financial boom that the stockyards brought the city played no small part in the tremendous growth that the city experienced in the late 19th century, turning it from a minor city into one of the great metropolitan centers of the western world, and earning the city its later nickname of "Hog Butcher for the World."

The stockyards had also become something of a tourist attraction for the city, and thousands of tourists came to see the facilities that were preparing more than 80 percent of the meat consumed in the country. John B. Sherman, the superintendent, even commissioned John Root of Burnham and Root, perhaps the most influential architects in the city, to design and create the ornate limestone gates that stood at the entrance, crowned by the bust of a head of cattle nicknamed "Sherman" and said to be modeled on the appearance of one of Mr. Sherman's own prized heads of cattle. A portion of the gate still stands on the site.

But there was, without question, a distinct dark side to the work and prosperity at the yards. Though the yards provided a lot of jobs, most of these were not particularly *good* jobs. Pay was low and benefits practically non-existent. The work was not only long and tedious, but often dangerous, and frequently hazardous to employees' health. And, if a job made an employee sick, the company was not about to cover the medical bills.

And stories circulated from an early date about how unsanitary the place was—a popular rhyme went:

Mary had a little lamb
and when she saw it sicken
she sent it off to Packingtown
it came back labeled "chicken."

Even from outside, people could see that the stockyards were by no means a pleasant place—the odor of the slaughterhouses could be smelled miles away. At one point 500,000 gallons of water from the Chicago River were being pumped into the yards a day, and so much waste from the yards was drained back in that the south fork of the river actually began to bubble from all the decomposing waste. This was a major concern for the city—when the city reversed the flow of the river, forcing it flow outward towards St. Louis instead of into Lake Michigan, as it had previously done (in a remarkable feat of engineering), a primary purpose was to keep the waste from the stockyards out of the drinking water.

In 1904, a young author named Upton Sinclair walked up to the gates

Cover of an early edition of Upton Sinclair's *The Jungle*

of Chicago's famous "Packingtown," the stockyards where a huge portion of the meat consumed in the United States was processed. Rumors and stories had gone around for years about outrageously unsanitary conditions in the yards, but the owners were adept at making sure reporters and inspectors saw only what they wanted them to see. By showing up dressed in shabby work clothes and carrying a lunch bucket, Sinclair found that no one stopped him from going anywhere on the grounds. Anyone who saw him just assumed he was one of the thousands of employees and had a good reason to be there.

Sinclair ended up spending about six months investigating conditions in the stockyards and meeting with the people who worked there. He was appalled by what he found. The unsanitary conditions in the stockyards were horrific, the lives of those who worked in them were wretched, and if the public at large knew the half of what was done to their meat, they probably wouldn't want to eat another bite of it.

Rather than presenting his findings in an essay or report, Sinclair used what he learned to write *The Jungle*, a novel that was first published serially in a newspaper throughout 1905. The novel told the story of a young immigrant and his family, and how they were abused by employers who broke their hearts and their bodies for financial gain, all the while caring nothing about the health of their customers.

Sinclair, a Socialist, had hoped that the novel would inspire people to rise up against capitalism altogether, but it didn't quite work out that way. They didn't rise up against "the system" so much as the idea of eating dirty meat. "I aimed at the public's heart," he told a magazine, "and by accident hit it in the stomach." When the novel became a sensation, meat sales plummeted, and President Theodore Roosevelt, who agreed with Sinclair that action against the meat industry was necessary, pushed through the Pure Food and Drug Act, as well as the Meat Inspection Act.

The stockyard managers tried their best to continue shirking the regulations in the face of the new laws; meatpackers were put to work three shifts a day for three weeks cleaning the factories ahead of the inspections they knew were coming. Even after all that work, though, inspectors sent by Roosevelt found them to be in loathsome condition (though they found nothing to substantiate some of Sinclair's wilder claims, such as the story about workers dying in rendering vats and being made into lard for sale to the public).

Sinclair, for his part, was not at all satisfied by the new legislation, particularly because the tens of millions that would be spent on inspections were to be paid by taxpayers, not by the owners of the meatpacking companies themselves.

Still, once the reforms were put in place, public confidence in the quality of the meat they were eating soared, and sales returned to their previous rates. The stockyards continued to be a major Chicago landmark for more than half a century. By the end of World War II, though, the transportation world had changed. Advances in trucking and railroad cars changed the way meat was shipped, and stockyards became less necessary. By the end of the 1950s, many of the major packing companies were no longer using centralized stockyards at all, opting instead to have the livestock slaughtered closer to the farms. The stockyards officially closed down in 1971,

Swift & Co.'s Packing, c. 1905

Union Stockyard Gate, 1907

though a couple of meat packing plants still operate in the area, and the stockyard gates are still present on Exchange Avenue at Peoria Street, having been designated a National Historic Landmark in 1981. Just behind the gates stands a monument to every Chicago firefighter killed in the line of duty, with particular attention paid to the "fallen 21," the 21 soldiers who died in a fire at the stockyards in 1910, which would be the deadliest event for firefighters in the United States until the terrorist attacks on September 11, 2001.

OLD COWPATH

Just west of Clark Street on Monroe is an alley said to be an old cowpath. In the mid-20th century, cows were often led down the path to promote the livestock shows at the stockyards. Laws banning livestock from the Loop had to be temporarily waived!

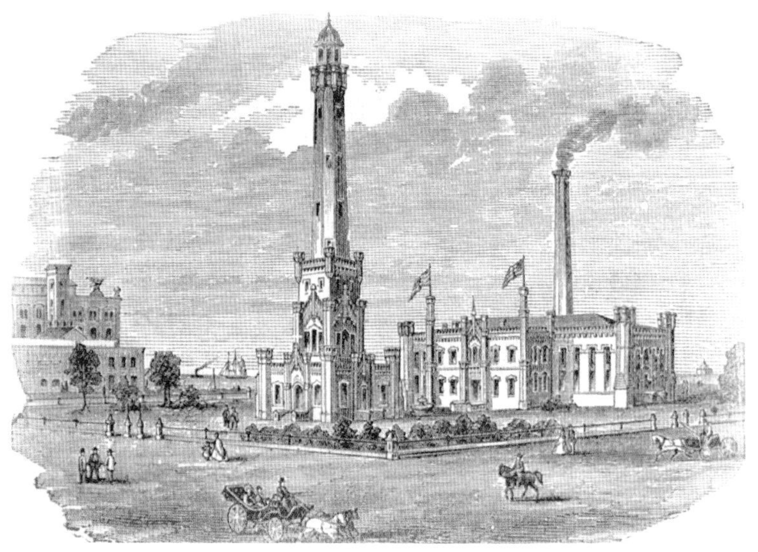

OLD CHICAGO SCENE: Water Tower and Chicago Avenue Pumping Station, c. 1886

ALL RAILROADS MEET IN CHICAGO

Maybe Senator Douglas was just being selfish when he lobbied for Chicago to become a hub for the Illinois Central Railroad—he owned land in Chicago, and a major railroad coming into town would make that land more valuable. Then again, he also thought that a railroad running from Chicago down to the Gulf of Mexico would help the north and south work together, easing the regional tensions that were threatening to tear the country apart in the 1850s.

Whatever the reason, the growth of railroads in the city helped Chicago triple its population in the 1850s, going from about 30,000 to more than 100,000.

Situated right on a major lake, near the new Illinois Michigan Canal, and right in the heart of the nation, Chicago began as a major hub both for north-south lines and east-west lines, and soon became the most important railroad hub in the nation.

This happened almost overnight. Although Chicago was known as an important railroad city as early as 1850, only one went through town at the time, the Galena and Chicago Union (which, oddly, didn't actually go to Galena). By the end of 1852, there were five railroads in town, and another five had been added by the end of the decade.

Initially the railroads were only meant to haul freight across the nation—farmers could ship their produce cheaper by rail than by steamboat, leading to greater distribution and lower prices. But soon, the railroads began adding passenger service as well, bringing people into the growing city by the thousands. By 1860, the city was large and important enough to host the Republican Convention that nominated Abraham Lincoln for the presidency. It might be that Lincoln, a candidate who came out of nowhere, could never have been nominated anywhere else (Illinois gave him a home-field advantage). His

Freight train operations on the Chicago and Northwestern Railroad, 1943

presidency could never have come to pass if it were not for the growth of the railroads.

The golden age of railroads might be over today, but Chicago is still among the most important railroad cities in the United States, with more lines stretching out in more directions than any other city, and trains still play a huge role in the hustle and bustle of the town. Chicago is second only to New York in the number of daily commuters who come in by train from the suburbs, and the El trains that ferry passengers through the city are an essential part of the daily life of millions of Chicago residents. Chicago also remains a major hub for Amtrak, and plans are in place for a new high-speed midwestern rail service that will connect Chicago to other major cities via trains traveling as fast as 110 miles per hour.

The Metra trains connect the city to the suburbs; indeed, many of the suburbs grew simply because the railroad gave people a chance to commute from the city out to more spacious areas. Towns like Naperville, La Grange, and Downer's Grove still have railroad stops right in the heart of central downtowns—surrounded by the elegant Victorian mansions built by the original commuters more than a century ago.

A local favorite train to ride in the city is the Brown Line El train, which circles around the Loop, giving passengers a wonderful view of the Magnificent Mile and some of the finest skyscrapers downtown, then heads through the north side, granting passengers a view of the brick townhouses, tree-lined streets, chimneys and rooftops of the Gold Coast, Lakeview, Lincoln Square and Ravenswood. If you get on in the morning, the outbound trains are usually uncrowded, since most of the commuter traffic is heading inbound.

Step off at the Armitage Stop and wander through the Armitage-Halsted historic district. The Belmont stop is close to several quirky shops and restaurants, and leaves you only a short hike from Wrigley Field. Get off at Western and enjoy the shops, bakeries and "Old Europe" atmosphere of Lincoln Square.

CHAPTER 6.

THE GREAT CHICAGO FIRE: THE TRAGEDY THAT BECAME A NEW BEGINNING

1871

Many newspapers in the 19th century were known to dabble in racism, but *The Chicago Times*, edited by Wilbur F. Storey, positively reveled in it. In the Civil War, the *Times* was Chicago's anti-Lincoln newspaper, publishing slanderous claims that Lincoln was going to séances for advice on the war from the spirit of his old rival, Senator Stephen Douglas. Union General Ambrose Burnside tried to shut Storey's paper down, and when Lincoln ordered the ban lifted, Storey responded by writing lyrics to a new song that presented himself as a crusader for "white rights."

When the Civil War ended in 1865, Storey found himself adrift; even *he* wasn't cruel enough to slander Lincoln after his assassination (or, at the very least, he was astute enough to realize that if he did, he'd probably be run out of town on a rail). But when the Great Chicago Fire wiped out the city in 1871, Storey found a new group to slander: The Irish. He was only too happy to help spread the legend that the fire had started because Mrs. Catherine O'Leary had foolishly left a kerosene lantern next to her cow in the barn.

---

56 The Great Fire of Chicago. Scene from Frank Leslie's illustrated newspaper, 1871 Oct. 28

Vol. XXXIII.] NEW YORK, OCTOBER 28, 1871. [Price, 10 Cents. $4 00 Yea 13 Weeks

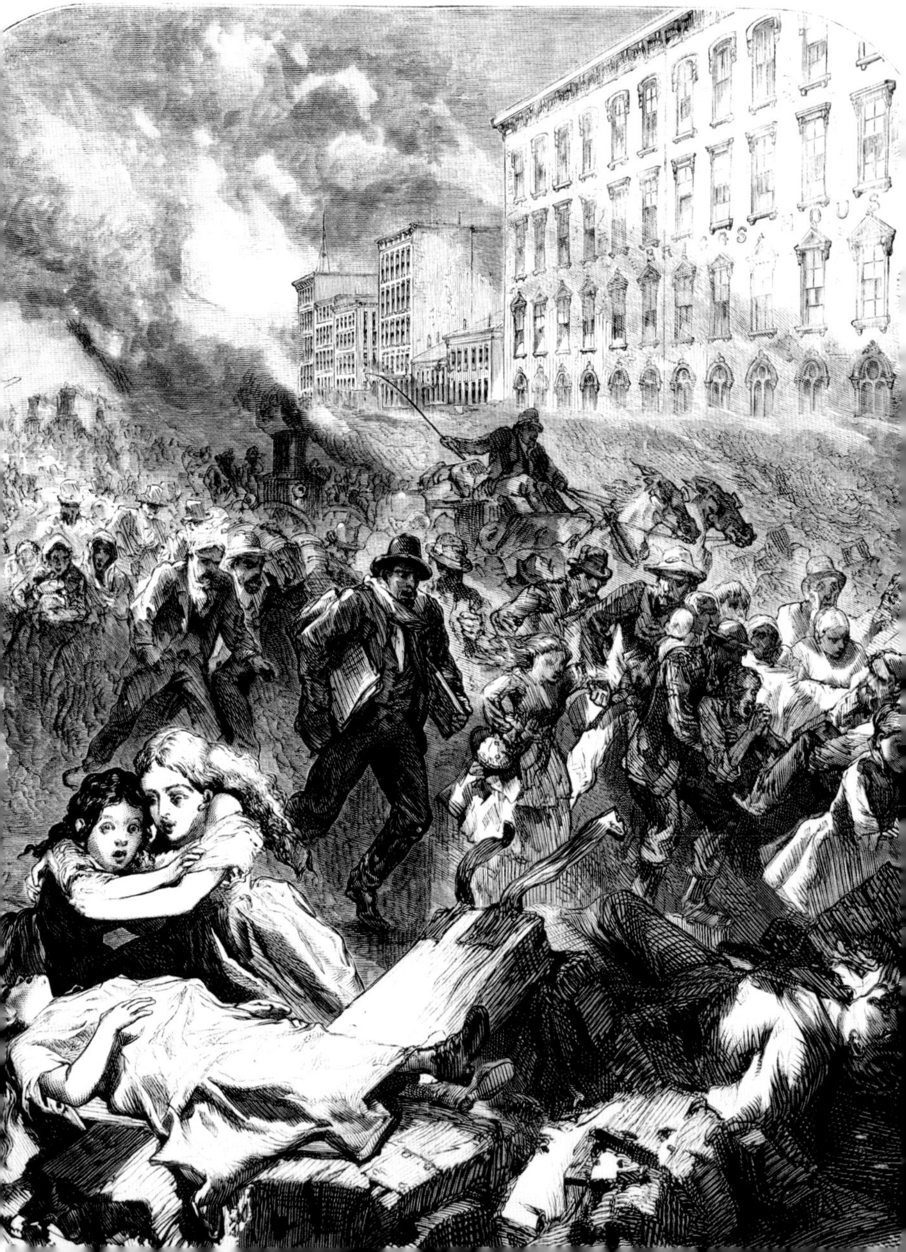

The Rush for Life Over the Randolph Street Bridge, Harper's Weekly, 1871

Exactly where that story got started isn't really known—Michael Ahern, a *Chicago Republican* reporter, claimed to have made it up on the 40th anniversary of the fire—but the newspapers certainly ran with it. Storey even claimed that she had started the fire on purpose. Papers all over spoke about her in cruel terms; the *Tribune* referred her and her neighbors' lack of solid information as to the origin of the fire as "Irish know-nothingness."

The exact *true* cause of the fire is still the subject of much debate. Some people believe it was started by a meteor that was also blamed for starting an even larger fire in Peshtigo, Wisconsin, the same day. Others say that it was the result of anarchist "incendiaries," a theory more popular in the old days than it seems to be now. Mrs. O'Leary's son, who grew up to be a notorious gambler known as "Big Jim," always blamed it on some sort of mysterious green hay that, he said, had spontaneously combusted in the barn.

Because of its rapid growth, the city was attracting the attention of the world, and rapidly becoming one of the most important cities in the United States, with a population that surpassed 330,000. The city had grown so quickly in the years before the fire that no one really had time to keep up with building codes; the buildings were rising faster than the city could inspect them.

"Fifty years ago," the *Tribune* wrote on the fire's first anniversary, "(Chicago)'s total obliteration would not have caused a moment's sensation in the outside world." But now things were different. Chicago was barely a mudhole in 1821, but by 1871 it was a major metropolis. Unfortunately, it was a major metropolis built largely of wood.

Whatever the cause, the fire broke out near the O'Leary family barn on the night of October 8, 1871. The barn stood on DeKoven Street, a narrow lane in which the wooden houses stood perilously close to the road, and the fire had no difficulty spreading. A fire engine arrived within 10 minutes, but by then the fire was far too large for a single engine; howling winds had carried the flames throughout the neighborhoods, and they were swallowing the nearby buildings and sheds that made up the West Division.

Even the addition of two more engines was not enough to fight the spread of the fire, and the flames marched northward in two parallel columns. One by one, residents of houses in the vicinity ran screaming from their homes, clutching their valuables and looking for a safe place to hide them. But there was no safe place. By midnight the fire had reached the "Loop" area, then, as now, the main downtown center, and was still spreading to the north, destroying everything in its path. All but a few prisoners of the jail at Clark and Washington were released; the most serious offenders were transferred to other prisons farther west, but minor offenders found themselves set free to find a safe place away from the fire.

By Monday morning, the fire had burned up most of the city west of Dearborn Street, and had stretched as far north as the Chicago River. McVicker's Theatre and the Palmer House Hotel initially appeared to be passed over by the flames, but the fire came back for them, as though the flames were retracing their steps to make sure they didn't miss a single spot. Most hoped that the fire wouldn't be able to cross the river, but the wind carried the flames right across the water, and on

Monday morning the north side was ablaze, and citizens were running for their lives. Many ended up sheltering in the recently dug graves that still littered the old City Cemetery, which had not yet completed its transition to becoming Lincoln Park.

Lincoln Park finally marked the end of the fire's merciless advance. By then, the fire had blazed for more than 24 hours, from nine o'clock Sunday evening until midnight the following day, destroying a patch of land four miles long and nearly a mile wide. More than 17,000 buildings were destroyed. Marble walls were melted away, and the wooden buildings were so destroyed that in many areas there was a remarkable lack of ruins in the smoldering aftermath—just a wasteland that looked as though it had never been inhabited at all. Losses were estimated to be in the range of $300 million in 1872 money—that would equal into the high billions today, if adjusted for inflation. Only a few buildings remained standing in the fire zone at all, including the Water Tower on the north side (which was badly scorched, but still working) and part of the old court house and prison, which were kept in use despite the damage they sustained until new versions could be built.

The Cause of the Great Chicago Fire Oct. 9th 1871; Mrs. Catherine O'Leary milking Daisy, Kellogg & Buckeley, c. 1872

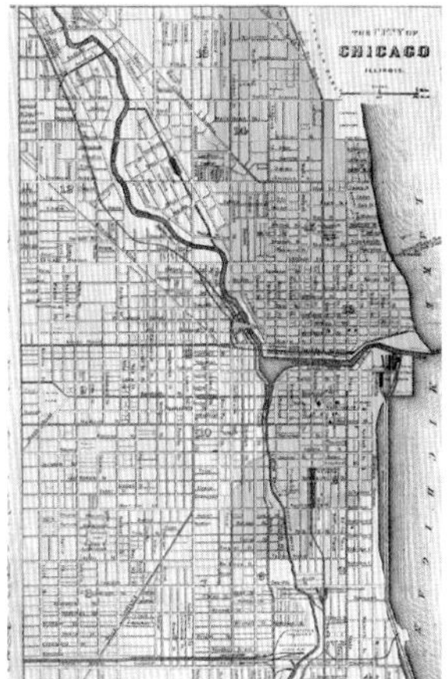

Map showing the burnt district of Chicago

The city didn't mourn its losses for long, but, with a gusto that amazed the world, began to rebuild. A sign posted in one area became the city's motto: "All gone but wife, children and energy." A popular story circulated about a man in a train station who was in a desperate hurry to see the ruins of Chicago before the city could be rebuilt.

But, in the midst of all the rebuilding, a scapegoat had to be found, and most people seemed to take Storey's tale of Mrs. O'Leary as fact. When Mrs. O'Leary refused to speak with reporters, even Storey's rivals at the *Tribune* referred to her "typical Irish know-nothingness." Though there was little evidence to connect her with the fire itself, she was brought to court and testified that her family was in bed, but not asleep, when the fire broke out, and that she had known nothing of it until a neighbor shouted that their barn was on fire. She had lost all of her property (a barn, wagons, several cows, and a horse), and had been so busy making sure her family was safe that she had had no time to look for clues as to the outbreak herself. The cow in question, however, was said to have survived, and was sold to a restaurant who served it up as oxtail soup.

Mrs. O'Leary's son later called the story "the monumental fake of the century," and Mrs. O'Leary developed, unsurprisingly, a deep dislike for reporters. In 1894, papers reported that "most people suppose (her) to be in the heavenly world, but (she) is still a resident of the city which she gets the credit of having burned to the ground. Her home is in the neighborhood of the stockyards, where she lives with her husband and her son at the good old age of 65, as happy as most people but extremely adverse to notoriety."

A family doctor tracked down by the press said "It would be impossible for me to describe to you the grief and indignation with which Mrs.

The rebuilding of the Marine Building, c. 1873

O'Leary views the place that has been assigned her in history. That she is regarded as the cause, even accidentally, of the great Chicago fire is the grief of her life. (The story) she attributes to the Chicago press, for which she entertains the bitterest hatred. She admits no reporters to her presence, and she is determined that whatever ridicule history may heap on her it will have to do it without the aid of her likeness. Many are the devices that have been tried to procure a picture of her, but she has been too sharp for any of them. No cartoon will ever make any sport of her features. She has not a likeness in the world and will never have one." A business owner even offered her a large sum of money simply to sit in his business while her husband did odd jobs, but the idea "Struck her with horror and disgust."

She got her wish about not having a likeness in the world—at the time of her death in 1895, no photograph had ever been taken of her. Today, the academy where firefighters are trained stands on the site of the old O'Leary property on Taylor Street, with a statue of the flame to mark the site of the fire's origin. In 1997, the city council exonerated her of all guilt and issued a formal apology—more than a century too late.

OLD CHICAGO SCENE: One of the busiest streets in the world—State St., N. from Madison St., c. 1903

CHAPTER 7.

LINCOLN PARK: HOW MANY CHICAGOANS KNOW THAT THEIR FAVORITE PARK WAS ONCE A GRAVEYARD?

1865

In 1998, workers digging out land for a new parking lot in the south end of Lincoln Park came across something they probably hadn't expected: a Fisk Metallic Burial Case. These metal coffins—ornately formed with a viewing window over the face—were all the rage in the 1850s, and this one contained a man who was in such good shape that they could still see his handlebar mustache—at least until the yellow excavator machine chopped through his feet.

Such a well-preserved corpse was a surprise, but the workmen had expected to find some human remains while they were digging. In fact, they found fragments of eighty more bodies whose coffins had long since rotted away while they were working. The sheer number was a bit of a surprise, but not too much of one. After all, it was well known that Lincoln Park had been the site of the City Cemetery for a good 20 years leading up to the end of the Civil War.

Years ago, people who died in cities were usually buried in churchyards. These got overcrowded very quickly; coffins were often stacked on top

of one another, and stories of workers having to jump up and down on top of the highest layer to keep them below the surface were common, as well as stories of not-quite-skeletal arms reaching from the ground, and of churchgoers passing out from the smell during services in the hotter months. So early Chicagoans made the rather progressive decision to put aside a couple of patches of land for burials. The first were at the present-day site of Chicago Avenue, near Michigan, around where the water tower now stands, and in a plot of land near what is now 26th Street on the shore of Lake Michigan. At the time, no one believed that many people would ever live north of the Chicago River. But as the city spread, the cemetery was moved northward, and eventually in 1842, a large plot of land on the north side—the future Lincoln Park—was set aside for cemetery use, and burials began there the next year. It is estimated that some 50,000 burials took place there between 1843 and the end of the Civil War in 1865, including roughly 5,000 Confederate prisoners of war who died at Camp Douglas, the prison camp that stood on the south side.

Eventually, as more and more people began to live farther north from the Loop, the proximity of the cemetery to both the new residences and the water pumping stations began to worry people, which resulted in the cemetery closing in the 1860s. Bodies were dug up and moved elsewhere—there were still some open graves during the Great Fire in 1871 that became convenient hiding places for people escaping from the flames.

Lincoln Memorial, executed by St. Gaudens, Lincoln Park, c. 1908

Today, no one is entirely sure how many bodies were left behind. At the south end of the park, one major monument still stands: the tomb of

The Burning of Chicago: Rush of fugitives through the Potter's Field toward Lincoln Park, 1871, *Harper's Weekly;* and David Kennison

the Couch Family, built in 1858 when Ira Couch died. Ira and his brother, James, had owned the Tremont House, a massive hotel at Dearborn and Lake that hosted both Abraham Lincoln and John Wilkes Booth (at different times, of course).

The tomb cost $7,000 to construct—roughly 20 years salary for many workers at the time—and it is generally thought that it was never moved simply because the city didn't want to spend the $3,000 it would cost to move such a large tomb. According to a later article, an attempt to inter James Couch there after his death in the 1890s—by which the transition from cemetery to park was otherwise complete—was thwarted only because the door had rusted shut. The door is still well-sealed today, and no one is sure how many bodies, if any, are currently inside of the tomb, though Ira's grandson estimated that there were about eight of them in the early 20th century.

A block north of the infamous parking lot sits one other reminder of the park's history—a memorial boulder marking the burial place of David Kennison. At the time of Kennison's death, he was one of the first heroes of Chicago, and a citizen that every Chicagoan was proud to call a neighbor. He had told everyone that he was 115 years old, and that he was the last surviving participant of the Boston Tea Party, in addition to the many honors he had earned fighting in various battles in both

Shore Drive, Lincoln Park, c. 1905

the Revolution and the War of 1812. When he died, he was given a full military funeral, and a vial of tea leaves he said were from Boston were given to the Chicago Historical Society. They still have them in their collection—even though we now know that Kennison was really more of a con artist than a war hero. He wasn't anywhere near as old as he claimed, and if he had been present at the Boston Tea Party, he would have been riding on his father's shoulders.

However, in the 1890s, the people of Chicago hadn't yet learned this. As Lincoln Park began to flourish, people began to feel bad that the body of an American hero was now lying in an unmarked grave somewhere in the cemetery (apparently, no one even suggested that he had actually been moved). A group of old timers who had been present at his funeral were rounded up, and the group determined, based on their memories, where in the park he had been buried. They were wrong; modern research indicates that they pinpointed the spot where the funeral occurred, but the burial actually took place a block south a few days later. A boulder with a plaque about Kennison's life was placed on the funeral spot, and still stands today—even though we now not only know that the location is not his actual burial place, but that his stories were mostly nonsense.

Aerial overview of Lincoln Park along North Lake Shore Drive, after 1969

Beyond these artifacts, though, one would be hard-pressed to find any evidence today that Lincoln Park was ever a grim and solemn place. The baseball and softball fields are active, the lagoon is gorgeous, and the park is perfect for picnics. Amenities include more than a dozen baseball areas, 35 tennis courts, several basketball courts, more than 100 volleyball courts, a lakeside theater, and a wonderful conservatory.

LINCOLN PARK ZOO

Lincoln Park Zoo, c. 1901

At the north end of the park is one of Chicago's most delightful attractions—the Lincoln Park Zoo, home to more than 1,000 animals, as well as a burr oak tree that dates back to 1830, three years before the town was incorporated.

The first animals for the zoo were a pair of swans that were given to the city in 1868, well before the transition from cemetery to park was complete. The first animal purchased specifically for the zoo was a bear that was purchased in 1874.

In the early days of the zoo, there was considerable trouble with animals escaping from their cages and habitats. Jim the Hyena, said to be as big as a lion and twice as ferocious, escaped in 1897 and made his way to Graceland Cemetery, where he jumped from the bushes and scared a night watchman out of his wits. For several days, Jim raced through the cemetery, eluding several hunters and scaring mourners. After breaking out of the cemetery, he terrified the north side for more than a week before being caught near a home for the elderly in the north suburbs.

The hyena wasn't the only trouble. In 1899, a new Russian cinnamon bear was brought to the park, and was clearly not used to having baths—when a hose was turned on him he broke away from the habitat, running more than a mile through the north side before he was caught.

One of the zoo's most famous residents was Bushman, a gorilla named for silent film idol Francis X. Bushman, who made a career for himself working at Essanay, the studio on the city's north side. Bushman was beloved by a generation of Chicagoans, and after his 1951 death, his stuffed remains were given to the Field Museum, where they have been on permanent display ever since. The fact that this gorilla had a "permanent" name at all was remarkable—in the early days of the zoo, one of the zoo's favorite promotions was to allow visiting celebrities to name an animal at the park, but the names rarely stuck. One lion was variously known as "Teddy Roosevelt" and "Whiskers" by the various tamers, and, according to a 1903 article, most of the animals were usually just called "Bill."

Even now, the zoo animals are far from the only wildlife in Lincoln Park—coyotes have recently been sighted in the park. But the occasional sightings of wildlife haven't kept people away from the gorgeous nature walk, the zoo (which is free to the public), or the popular farmers markets, which operate on Wednesdays and Saturdays in the summer and fall.

CHAPTER 8.

CAPTAIN STREETER: BARELY A CENTURY AGO THE MAGNIFICENT MILE WAS STILL CALLED SHANTYTOWN

1886-1918

When you drive up Lake Shore Drive around the Magnificent Mile today, you're walking over an old garbage heap. And not just any garbage heap, but the one that Captain George Wellington Streeter had claimed as his own country. The claim may sound absurd, but he managed to hang on to it for a good 30 years after forging a few documents in the late 1880s.

In the 1910s and 20s, the area near the water tower was known as Towertown, the bohemian capitol of the city. If you wandered down Tooker Alley, a narrow passageway off State Street, you would come to a door reading "Step high, stoop low, and leave your dignity outside." This was the entrance to the Dil Pickle Club, where the artists, intellectuals and radicals came to play. In addition to musical and theatrical performances, owner Jack Jones tried to line up interesting speakers every night, "anyone who was a nut about something." Yellow Kid Weill, a notable con man, spoke there one night and demonstrated his powers by conning the audience out of 20 bucks.

 The Magnificent Mile runs from the Chicago River Bascule Bridge at North Michigan Avenue to Oak Street

The front door of the Dil Pickle Club at 18 W. Tooker Place

In July, 1919, Jones landed a real coup by booking Captain George Wellington Streeter, himself. His "Thirty Years War" with the city was over—he had been removed from the landfill that he claimed as an independent country. But he still had a story to tell.

The "Cap'n" arrived an hour late, and shuffled to the front of the room, in his trademark plug hat. "I'm glad to see you all, ladies and gen'lmen," he said. "I haven't made up my mind what I'm goin' to talk about, but...."

And from there, he launched into a long monologue in which he discussed "everything but girth control and the ethical code of the dinosaurs," according to one witness. He retold the many battles he had survived against the police in his "thirty years war." "People oughtn't be dragged off to prison for arguin'," he said. "That's what they done in Ireland, an' what is the result? The Irish is just as bad as ever."

The crowd ate the performance up. And why shouldn't they? This was Cap Streeter, the "last pioneer" of Chicago, whose antics had been fodder for the newspapers for decades.

In the old days, Lake Michigan went all the way out to Michigan Avenue in the downtown area. In fact, this was why they called it Michigan Avenue. After the Great Fire in 1871, rubble from the fire was used to create a landfill west of downtown; this was the land that became Grant Park. North of that, the city planned to add more land to create Lake Shore Drive, the great boulevard that would run alongside the city a half mile west of the edge of town, in what was, at the time, the middle of the lake.

In the midst of the planning and preparations, Captain George Streeter crashed his houseboat onto the shore just north of the Loop in 1886.

Though the process of filling in the land had already begun, he declared himself the owner of the new space, and, using his own particular gifts as a con artist, started charging people money to dump their garbage around his boat.

When the 186-acre landfill was complete, Streeter declared that he was the owner of the land and forged himself a couple of deeds. He went to court holding a letter signed by several lawyers backing up his claim. None of them had actually signed it; Streeter had just gone around the city looking at the names of lawyers on signs outside of their offices, then forged their signatures. He once even forged the signature of President Grover Cleveland on a deed.

The claim might, in fact, have had some merit. The city had officially been granting ownership of the new land to whoever owned the land adjacent to it, and the legal right to do this was shaky, at best. Taking advantage of the momentary confusion, Streeter discovered an old map of the city showing that the City of Chicago's land only extended to the original shoreline, meaning that any new land that "appeared" to the west of the shore was not legally within the city's jurisdiction.

Captain Streeter with his wife, sitting in front of their home with their dog, 1915

The District of Lake Michigan, 1909, and Captain Streeter with his boat, the Reutan

Assuming that the new land was also out of the control of the state of Illinois, and, therefore, out of the hands of the United States of America, Captain Streeter declared that the new land was his own country, The District of Michigan, and began to sell lots on the land to hobos who emigrated to his new country. Before long, the wealthy owners of Lake Michigan mansions who previously had an unobstructed view of Lake Michigan now had unobstructed views of shacks and shanties that served as gambling halls, brothels, whiskey bars and apartments. There was no indoor plumbing, and few outhouses, so they were also treated to delightful views of hobos using chamber pots.

Naturally, neither the wealthy mansion owners nor the city officials were happy about this—lakefront property just north of the Loop was incredibly valuable, and Streeter's bravado kept them from removing him, no matter how tenuous his claims were. "By all that's living, you can't take me," he'd shout.

And they couldn't take him, either. For 30 years, the battle dragged on, both in the form of legal battles and actual gunfights between the police and the army of hobos the captain had built up—and "Streeter's Army" was known to fight dirty. They were not above attacking invaders with the contents of chamber pots. One associate said that Streeter preferred fighting to eating.

By the end of the battle, the stories the Captain told about his long struggle were such a broad mix of fact and fiction that it was impossible to know how much of it was true. In 1918, though, the court officially decided that any claim he had ever had was fictitious and evicted him from the land. He sailed his houseboat south, and for a time made a living for himself by selling coffee from a cart around what is now Navy Pier.

Three years later, the captain died and was buried with something close to military honors at Graceland Cemetery, and his supporters vowed to carry on the fight for control of his "Deestrict." For a time, Jack Jones of the Dil Pickle became president of Streeterville, and actually marched onto the beach to order bathers to disperse. He planned to use the land to build homes for disabled veterans of World War I, chapels for odd religious sects, an art center, a literary center, and a 10-story building full of apartments to be rented to families with children. In contrast to Streeter's 30-year fight, Jones's insurrection didn't last 30 minutes. Police told him to "beat it" and chased him off.

Within a decade, the "Deestrict" had been built over, and was a part of the area soon known as "The Magnificent Mile." By 1931, newspapers were calling it "one of the world's most miraculous shopping districts," and the "miracle" was that it had been built where there had only been shacks and beaches a mere decade before. Luxurious hotels and high rises now poked toward the sky. The *Tribune* described a typical night scene in the "Deestrict" in 1931: "Ladies in evening gowns come shining out of the taxis with their escorts. Buyers from out of town are piloted skillfully into the nightclubs, where professional hostesses expertly put them into the right frame of

Streeterville neighborhood building boom, 1925, *Field Artillery Journal*, 1926

Aerial view of downtown Chicago–Streeterville (left), late 1920s

mind to loosen up with the firm's money." It's hard to imagine a bigger contrast from the shantytown that had stood there only a few years before, and few of the nightclub-hoppers could imagine that they were dancing on top of a landfill.

It's even harder to believe now, when Streeter and his "Deestrict" have passed from living memory. Today more than ever, the near north side west of Lake Michigan, home of the Hancock Building and the luxurious townhouses that line Lake Shore Drive, is as plush as the city gets. On weekend nights the area is replete with nightclub-hoppers, late night shoppers, and couples riding in horse-drawn carriages to see a glimpse of "old Chicago."

The city still refers to the area as "Streeterville" in the Captain's honor, and in 2010 a bronze statue of Captain Streeter was installed outside of the Streeter Place apartments at Grand Avenue and McClurg Court. The statue stands eight feet tall, and features the Captain in his trademark hat, and carrying the dog from whom he was inseparable. Together, they keep an unending watch over the neighborhood they called their own.

OLD CHICAGO SCENE: F.M. Smith & Co., between 1895 and 1910

CHAPTER 9.

JANE ADDAMS: THE DEVIL BABY WHO MADE HULL HOUSE FAMOUS

1889

Jane Addams stood in shock, staring at the men who were standing on the porch of Hull House, the "settlement house" she'd been running on Chicago's west side for a quarter of a century.

"It must be here," said one.

"The women saw it," said another.
For weeks, a rumor had spread among the west side that somewhere inside of Hull House, Addams and her staff were hiding some sort of "Devil Baby." According to the rumor, some man in the neighborhood had said something to anger God, perhaps "I would rather have our next baby be the devil than another girl," or "I would rather have a devil in the house than one of that traveling salesman's fancy Bibles." And, the rumor went, he got his wish: his wife had given birth to a baby with scaly red skin, horns, hooves, and a tail. Some variations even had the minute-old baby smoking cigars, eating hot coals, and swearing in English, Latin and Italian. The stories told around the neighborhood varied in their details, but they all ended the same way: with the

 Press correspondents with Lillian Wald and Jane Addams, 1916

baby being brought to Hull House. In addition to the people of the neighborhood, reporters and even clergymen were descending on the house in droves.

Similar stories had circulated around other cities, as well, but in Chicago the story had changed: in most cities, people would descend on the house where the Devil Baby was said to live intending to kill it. At Hull House, people were offering to pay admission to see it.

Addams looked at the men in dismay.
"Do you really think," she said, "that even if we had some poor, deformed baby here, we would charge admission to see it?"

"Well, sure!" said one of them.

"It teaches a good lesson," said another.

Addams—who was certainly not harboring any such baby in the house—was left to reflect on how strange an institution Hull House must have seemed to the men. Situated in the "West Side" known for its slums and saloons, Hull House was a "settlement house," a place where people could come to arrange for day care, get counseling, learn English, take music lessons, and enjoy cultural programming to counter the entertainments offered in the saloons and brothels elsewhere in the neighborhood. It was a smashing success; Addams was famous throughout the world by 1913, and the operation had expanded from one building to a block-long complex.

Still, many neighbors never quite understood the place, and others were downright suspicious of it. It was a house full of women all living together, and their efforts to improve the lives of the neighbors were not all based around Bible study. The year before, Addams had become the first woman to address a major political convention when she seconded Theodore Roosevelt's nomination as the Bull Moose Party candidate during the campaign of 1912—Roosevelt (who eventually came in second, beating his old Republican Party but losing the election to Woodrow Wilson and the Democrats) had become the first major candidate to come out fully for women's suffrage. For years, people who

Applicants for Admission to a Casual Ward, Luke Fildes, 1874, Royal Holloway College, Egham, Surrey, UK

knew her had been saying "There's no one in the world like Miss Addams."

Addams was born to a prosperous family in western Illinois; her father was a good friend of Abraham Lincoln, who called him "My dear Mister double-D Addams" in the letters that the family treasured long after the president's death when Jane was four years old. Throughout her life, she dreamed of doing big things to improve the world, and her love of the works of Charles Dickens made her want to help the poor.

After her father's death, Addams inherited enough money to last her a lifetime, but didn't abandon her dream of helping the poor. She never finished medical school, her original plan, but moved to London and got work in Toynbee Hall, a settlement house that had been set up to help "raise up" the women of White Chapel, which was generally known to be the worst neighborhood in London at the time. She was thrilled by the atmosphere of the place: this was not a place for self-righteous "do gooders," but a place where educated, professional people lived and worked side by side with the poor, organizing libraries and recreation clubs "in the same style in which they would live in their own circle." Such mingling of the classes was, at the time, nearly unheard of.

Meanwhile, in 1888, Charles J. Hull, a real estate magnate, had died in Chicago leaving the whole of his estate, including the now run-down old mansion on Halsted, to his housekeeper, Helen Culver. The mansion had been on the edge of the prairie when it was built (an old painting makes it look like it was in the middle of the countryside), but now it was surrounded by slums; a saloon stood on one side of it, and an undertaking parlor stood on the other side. Culver was excited by

Children playing in Hull House, c. 1900

Addams's idea of starting a settlement house, and granted Addams a life-long, rent-free lease on the place.

Addams moved into the home with a few partners. Their initial plan was simply to invite the neighborhood women into their house to talk, but their efforts caught on quickly, and soon there were 25 full-time residents at the house, and its operations began to expand. A children's center with a nursery, kindergarten, and areas for children's clubs to meet was built in to replace the undertaking parlor next door. A theater and coffee shop replaced the saloon on the other side. Soon, there was also an art gallery, a coffee house (their most successful alternative to the saloons), a gym, a library, a night school for adults, a music school (where jazz legend Benny Goodman learned to play the clarinet) and other facilities spread across a 13-building complex that became the most famous settlement house in the world, and the inspiration for countless others that sprang up around the country.

The West Side was, at the time, a very poor area, inhabited largely by recent immigrants from Europe. When the "Devil Baby" story spread, Addams recognized that many of the women who were so excited by it saw the tale as a way to keep clinging to their old-world superstitions they had grown up with. Finding out that many of the things they had grown up believing were regarded as local superstitions everywhere else was a hard thing to accept. Addams loved folklore, personally, and collected anecdotes about superstitions and old-world beliefs surviving in America; she even found that the previous tenants of Hull House had set up buckets of water on top of the stairs, apparently due to a belief that the attic was haunted (a commonly held belief about the house to this day), but that the ghost couldn't cross over water.

So, as annoyed as she was by the throngs looking for the demon child, she saw some value in the story, and particularly saw the value it held for the women who came to her door. These were women who had little control over their own lives. Many were abused by their husbands, and neglected by their successful children, who often grew up to think that their "old world" parents were an embarrassment. Many had survived unspeakable hardships. The Devil Baby story gave them hope that God would punish cruel husbands; one hallmark in all of the variations of the rumor was that God seemed more interested in punishing the husband than protecting the wife, but that was good enough for many of them. It was something.

By 1913, when the Devil Baby rumor took the city by storm, Addams was already very famous; she had been on several lecture tours, and her 1912 book, *Twenty Years at Hull House*, was one of the most widely read books of the day. Soon, she was speaking about the Devil Baby story in lectures and in books. Everything that happened in the neighborhood became fuel for more activism for Addams.

In 1915, she became national chairman of the Women's Peace Party, which worked to find a way to end World War I. That made some call her "unpatriotic," but the work she did for peace eventually led to her being the first American woman to win the Nobel Peace Prize, an honor she was given in 1931.

Exterior of the Hull House Settlement, c. 1910

Even after her death in 1936, Hull House remained a force for good in Chicago for several decades until the Hull House Foundation

Peace delegates on the Noordam: Mrs. P. Lawrence, Jane Addams, Anna Molloy, 1915

closed down in 2012. After the main operations were moved from the original site in the 1950s, most of the original Hull House buildings were removed, leaving only the dining hall and the original mansion, which was restored to look the way it would have when Jane Addams first moved in. The University of Illinois built its Chicago campus around the old mansion, which became a museum dedicated to Jane Addams's life and work. The extensively restored house is one of very few structures in the general downtown area that survives from the days before the Great Chicago Fire, which spared the house, though it started only blocks away. It's a strange sensation to stand on the porch, looking at the nearby skyline, and reflect on the fact that the house was once on the very edge of the city.

THE OLD HULL HOUSE

"The Old Hull House" was only about 30 years old when Addams moved in, but looked much older, and stood out like a sore thumb in the neighborhood of slums and shacks. It was already reputed to be haunted as early as 1889, a reputation that survives today.

JANE ADDAMS HULL HOUSE MUSEUM

In the 1960s, after the main operations of Hull House were moved elsewhere, the original house was restored, and is now home to a museum celebrating Addams, her work, and her era. Located in the restored house at 800 South Halsted, it is open Tuesday through Friday from 10am to 4pm, and Sundays from noon to 4pm. Admission is free.

CHAPTER 10.

BATHHOUSE JOHN, HINKY DINK KENNA, AND THE FIRST WARD BALL: CROOKED POLITICS BECOMES GREAT ENTERTAINMENT

1896-1908

You have probably never heard the songs "Dear Midnight of Love," "Why Did They Make Lake Michigan So Wide" or "She Sleeps by the Side of the Drainage Canal." And, having read those titles, you can probably already guess that you aren't missing much. But a whole generation of Chicago's reporters and various representatives of the underworld not only had to *hear* these songs, they had to pretend they liked them. The author was Bathhouse John Coughlin, the eccentric old alderman of the First Ward.

Aldermen are like mayors of neighborhoods, and in the old days, each neighborhood had two of them. No pair was more famous or more corrupt, than "Bathhouse John" Coughlin and Michael "Hinky Dink" Kenna, the aldermen of the notorious "First Ward," a hotbed of crime, corruption and vice that sat a mile or two south of the Loop. It was in this neighborhood that Big Jim Colosimo became one of the city's first kingpins of organized crime, where his protégé John Torrio turned vice into an empire, and where *his* protégé, Al Capone, took over the empire that Torrio built after Colosimo's inevitable murder in 1920 (by most

Dear Midnight of Love
Words and Music
BY
JOHN J. COUGHLIN

accounts, he told Torrio that he didn't want to get involved in bootleg liquor after Prohibition took effect, and had to be taken out, but the mystery of his murder was never actually solved, like most murders in the First Ward).

It was also here, only blocks away, that Minna and Ada Everleigh ran the famous Everleigh Club. It would not be fair to call the Everleigh a "house of ill repute," because it had a fantastic reputation. Though the levy was riddled with both low-down brothels and classier ones, the Everleigh Club was in a class by itself. Housed in a stately mansion that was redecorated regularly, the brothel featured two of its own orchestras, full-time professional chefs who were the equal of any in the city, and a library for the education of the girls (though one upper-class patron famously snorted that "that's educating the wrong end of a whore"). Countless stories circulated about the place, such as a rumor that a customer who spent less than $50 (the equivalent of well over a thousand in modern currency) in an evening would be banned for life (true), and one that after a worker left a handprint on the wall, one of the "Sisters Everleigh" called in a painter to cover it up; when she told him "let me show you where a man put his hand last night," he paused

Chicago's levee district at night, published in *Harper's Weekly*, 1898

James Colosimo (left) sits with attorney Charles E. Erbstein in 1914 and Michael "Hinky Dink" Kenna

for a moment and said "if it's all the same to you, I'll just have a glass of beer." (this one may or may not be true, but it's a wonderful story).

Nearly every kind of vice was permitted in the First Ward, which was commonly known as "The Levee." Shouldered against such places as the Everleigh and Colosimo's Cafe were such delightfully named spots as The Bucket of Blood and Bed Bug Row. Crime ran rampant, and criminals plied their trade with something approaching immunity as long as they made their payments to Bathhouse John and Hinky Dink Kenna.

Hinky Dink was a no-nonsense type, despite his bizarre name, but Bathhouse John was full of enough nonsense for both of them. In addition to the "songs" he wrote (or took credit for when a reporter wrote them as a joke), he published a whole book of poems in 1908. Copies are hard to come by, but some of the poems, such as "Ode to a Bowl of Soup" survive, unfortunately. Consider, for instance, this "canto" from "Ode to a Bath Tub":

Some go to ball games for pleasure, others go bobbing for eels.
Some find delight making money, especially in real estate deals.
I care not for ball games or fishing, or money unless to buy grub
But I'd walk forty miles before breakfast to roll in the porcelain tub.

From left: Interior of one of the rooms at the Everleigh Club, designed to resemble a Pullman dining railroad car, 1909; Minna and Ada Everleigh

Did anyone ever really go bobbing for eels for fun?

If that doesn't stink enough for you, try this verse from "Under the Twinkling Stars":

She told me that she loved me as I held her hand in mine;
her lips were like to cherries of the Maraschino kind.
I drew her to my bosom, breaking two good cigars
and plucked the cherries from her lips—under the twinkling stars.

Now, imagine having to take these songs seriously. And not just that, but imagine having to tell Bathhouse John that you thought he was really a great poet—The Bard of the Levee. If you were a reporter or a First Ward resident in Bathhouse John's long era as alderman, you wouldn't have had a choice. Bathhouse John might have been an oaf who took credit for terrible poetry, published lists of the most handsome men in town, offered cash prizes to the first person to see a robin in spring, tirelessly promoted "straw hat day" every year, and wandered around town dressed in a bright green suit made of pool table felt, but you certainly didn't want him angry with you. Bathhouse John could get people off the hook for murder; and he and Hinky Dink's iron grip on the ward was absolute.

And no prominent citizen of the city dared not to buy a ticket to the

First Ward Ball, the annual orgy of corruption that they hosted at the old Coliseum. No one from the district they controlled dared miss the ball.

The First Ward Ball was sort of like today's Taste of Chicago Festival, the annual fest at which most of the major restaurants in the city offer samples of their wares to throngs of tourists while some of the most famous bands in the world provide entertainment. However, rather than restaurants, the exhibitors at the First Ward Balls were mostly professionals from the vice industry. A 1940 reminiscence of the balls in the *Tribune* wrote that "each December it assembled under one roof the madams and harlots, the robbers and killers, the pickpockets and footpads, the swindlers and thieves, and the drug addicts and common bums who made the levee infamous throughout the world."

The police came to the ball, too, and the cops and the criminals partied together in a sort of truce, all paying money into an event that was essentially a fundraiser for Bathhouse John's and Hinky Dink's campaign to keep their jobs in the next elections.

The first of the balls was held in the Seventh Regiment Armory building in 1896, though later balls were moved to the far larger Coliseum on Wabash. The highlight of the balls was the Grand March that Bathhouse John himself led at midnight, clad in his trademark green suit. Some say that Bathhouse John was never happier than in the moments when he led the march.

THE GRAND MARCH AT BATHHOUSE JOHN'S BALL

The Grand March at the First Ward Ball, John T. McCutcheon, *Chicago Tribune*, 1908

But Hinky Dink always said that the ball never really got exciting until

Convention crowd at the Coliseum, 1912

after 3a.m., when the fights broke out and all rules of decorum were set aside. By this hour, any hint that the ball had ever been a respectable gathering was forgotten, and one could see "unspeakable acts" of every description being practiced and demonstrated right out on the main floor.

It was these after-hours revels that really caught the attention of the reformers, and, though Coughlin stated that the 1908 ball would be the best one ever, the *Tribune* threatened to publish the name of every "respectable" citizen who attended. These "respectable" people were the ones who paid out the biggest money into Coughlin and Kenna's coffers, and few were willing to risk their reputations. Meanwhile, though Bathhouse and Kenna went ahead with their plans, the Coliseum was bombed by reformers, blowing out the windows.

Still, on the night of the ball, thousands packed the streets waiting to get in, and the party was one for the books. Three decades later, a reporter described it as "such a bedlam of thieves, robbers, plug uglies, dips, dope fiends, porch climbers and chronic bums and drunks as had never been gathered together since the days when the rabble of Rome were feted at the circuses." The crowd was packed so tightly that Kenna was forced to stage a bomb scare in order to get a large portion of the crowd to leave, making room for the Everleigh Sisters and their girls, who arrived at midnight with a police escort.

The vice commission published a report on the affair that was so bawdy that it was banned as "pornographic" by the United States post office. Many of the "respectable" people were scared away by the threats of the *Tribune* that year, and without their money, the ball was a financial failure. The next year, Coughlin and Kenna were forced to hold a "concert" instead, and few people wanted to come to any musical event that Bathhouse John was involved with.

Today, the levee district is unrecognizable. Now known as the "south Loop," the area is one of the hottest spaces for real estate in the country. Here and there you can see a vacant lot where Al Capone's Four Deuces club stood (2222 South Wabash), or a little park marking the space where the Coliseum was, but there are only a few buildings and scenes that can give any hint of what the neighborhood was like a century ago.

CHAPTER 11.

LOUIS SULLIVAN: PRESIDENT ROOSEVELT'S SPEECH AT THE ACOUSTICALLY PERFECT AUDITORIUM THEATRE

1903

April 2, 1903. A crowd of six thousand packed into the Auditorium Theatre on Congress and Michigan. Above the gallery was a mural with a quote line beneath reading "A great life has passed into the tomb / therein awaits the requiem of winter's snow." It was (and is) a remarkably somber sentiment for such an auditorium, especially on a day like April 2, 1903, when President Theodore Roosevelt kicked off the beginning of a 14,000-mile, 66 day tour, by far the most extensive trip ever taken by a sitting president. A flurried day of activities in Chicago ended with a jubilant speech at the Auditorium Theatre at 50 East Congress Parkway.

This speech would go down in history long after people forgot where, exactly, Roosevelt was when he uttered the famous words that would become his trademark, in a portion of the speech during which he admonished those whose idea of foreign policy was simply to make a lot of noise. "Boasting and blustering are as objectionable among nations as among individuals," he said. "There is a homely old adage which runs: 'speak softly and carry a big stick; you will go far.'"

 Grand banquet for President Roosevelt at the auditorium by the Iroquois Democratic Club of Chicago, May 10, 1905

ILLINOIS
U.S.
1776

Perhaps the most remarkable thing of all was that, in those days before microphones, people in the upper gallery, beneath the somber mural, could hear the President at all. But they could—and clearly. The Auditorium Theatre is still regarded today as an acoustically perfect auditorium; a speaker can stand on the stage and speak in a normal speaking voice, and people in the back row of the highest balcony can hear that speaker perfectly. They still demonstrate this on tours.

Completed in 1889, the Auditorium is one of the best surviving examples of a building designed by Louis Sullivan and Dankmar Adler. Sullivan is sometimes referred to as the father of the skyscraper, and was instrumental in creating many of the towering structures we see in Chicago today. His style is instantly recognizable on buildings with graceful, curving ornamental elements, such as the twisting Art Nouveau entrance of the Carson Pirie Scott Building on State Street (now the downtown Target store at 1 South State Street in the Loop). Although he coined the phrase "form follows function," which became a battle cry for a later generation of architects who built boring glass boxes, Sullivan was a designer who believed in the value of form. Many of his surviving buildings still look like works of art.

President Roosevelt's western tour, speaking in Evanston, Illinois, 1903

Dankmar Adler made Sullivan a partner in his firm when Sullivan was still in his early 20s, and the two made a name for themselves by designing a number of theaters in the early 1880s. The Auditorium was their biggest and most successful, including a hotel, an office, and storefronts in addition to the lush 4,200-seat theater. When completed, it was said to be the largest building in the

Louis Henry Sullivan, c. 1895 and Auditorium Theatre from Lake Michigan, *Harper's Weekly*, 1893

United States in terms of overall square footage.

The driving force behind having the complex built was businessman Ferdinand Peck, whose idea was to make high art accessible to the working classes. As such, he demanded that every seat be a good one, so that even people buying the cheapest seats could enjoy the grand operas that he envisioned the theater hosting. President Grover Cleveland laid the cornerstone for the building in 1887, and the next year the Republican National Convention nominated Benjamin Harrison to run against him there; the victorious President Harrison would formally dedicate the building the next year.

The Auditorium was thought to be the most expensive building ever built, but the money was put to good use—the Auditorium was a sight to behold. The interior (which included work by Sullivan's apprentice, Frank Lloyd Wright) included a mosaic floor containing more than a million hand-laid tiles. Murals were everywhere, including a "progression of man from birth to death" mural on the arch over the stage. The south gallery seats were crowned by a mural showing a springtime scene, with the words "O, soft, melodious spring time! First-born of life and love." The north gallery showed the same scene in late autumn, with the lines "A great life has passed into the tomb." The two were originally designed to be lit by a glass skylight that sat above them.

The temporary floor system allowed the theater to be used as a ballroom and a banquet hall, as well as a space for indoor sports

The Auditorium spent a few years as the jewel in Chicago's crown, hosting both the Chicago Symphony Orchestra and an opera company. But by the time the Great Depression came in the early 1930s, both the symphony and the opera company had moved to other venues, and the theater closed its doors. It was re-opened as a serviceman's center in World War II; soldiers were housed in the old hotel, and a bowling alley for their entertainment was set up on the old stage.

Though it was thought to be a "lost" theater in an era when the city was full of them (many of the great old theaters were reduced to showing low-rent B-movies or adult films by the 1970s), the acoustically perfect Auditorium was reborn in the late 1960s as a performance venue, and became the premiere venue in the city for rock concerts, hosting performances by Jimi Hendrix, The Doors, The Who, and Aretha Franklin. Today, the auditorium is a part of Roosevelt University and continues to host everything from rock concerts to the ballet. It is still magnificent.

Sullivan himself went on to bigger things, and was one of the architects chosen to help create the buildings for the Columbian Exposition, the massive World's Fair Chicago hosted in 1893. To his chagrin, many of the buildings were constructed in a Greek Revival style that so wowed visitors that Greek Revival became the style for municipal buildings. When you go to a small town anywhere in the country and see a post office with Greek-style pillars, it's likely there as a result of the influence of the World's Fair.

And Louis Sullivan hated that. He thought that a specific "American" style of architecture was just starting to emerge, and The World's Fair stopped it dead in its tracks, making small towns everywhere put up Greek Revival banks and post offices instead of something new and unique. There are exceptions, though, including a handful of small midwestern towns where Sullivan's own "jewel box" banks remain the centerpiece of the town square. To look at these buildings now, with Sullivan's signature ornamental stained glass fixtures, it's tempting to imagine how wonderful cities and towns might have looked if more of them had been designed with Sullivan's ethos; for decades, his position that the World's Fair ruined architecture was shared by a lot of designers.

Sullivan's own building on the fairgrounds was the Transportation Building, which, with its cascading arches and ornaments, is still instantly recognizable as a Sullivan building in photographs today, and must have stuck out like a sixth toe on the fairgrounds (it was, after all, the only non-white building in the "White City").

The view from the observation platform of the Manufacturers Building at World's Fair, Columbian Exposition, 1893

Following the Fair, and the financial panic of 1893 that came with it, Sullivan's career fell into decline, and he spent the next 30 years drinking himself to death, finally succumbing in a Chicago hotel room in 1924.

From left: The entrance of The Carson Pirie Scott building, The Russian Orthodox Church and Carrie Eliza Getty Tomb

A number of Sullivan buildings still stand in Chicago, such as the Jeweler's Building at 19 South Wabash Avenue, the Leon Mannheimer House at 2147 North Cleveland Avenue, The Carson Pirie Scott Building (now a Target store) on South State Street, and The Russian Orthodox Church at 1121 North Leavitt Street.

Perhaps the best surviving example of his style, though, is the tomb he designed for Carrie Eliza Getty, which sits not far from Sullivan's own resting place in Graceland Cemetery at 4001 North Clark Street. The massive limestone tomb features arches and stunning ornamental doors on which even the hinges are works of art. Frank Lloyd Wright called the Getty Tomb "entirely Sullivan's own, a piece of sculpture, a statue, a great poem."

THE AUDITORIUM

Today, you can walk through the building without going indoors. When Congress Parkway was widened in 1952, the building was not moved–the front of the building was simply hollowed out a little, so that the sidewalk now goes right through the old lobby. The building has been a National Historic Landmark since 1975, but is in no danger of disappearing and has no serious need for such protections, since the building is far too well built to be destroyed today; an attempt by developers to buy the land and tear down the theater went nowhere after it was discovered that it was so well built that tearing it down would be too expensive in and of itself to make any other venture on the spot profitable.

"FORM EVER FOLLOWS FUNCTION"

Perhaps Sullivan's best known quote about architecture is "Form ever follows function." He said it in an 1896 article publised in *Lippincott's Monthly Magazine* entitled "The Tall Office Building Artistically Considered."

After Sullivan came the era of Mies Van der Rohe and the "international" school of architects, who believed that "less is more." You can blame them for the buildings that look like plain glass boxes. Van der Rohe is buried at the same cemetery as Sullivan, and I like to imagine that their ghosts have a lot of arguments. And that Sullivan always wins.

WORLD'S COLUMBIAN EXPOSITION, 1893

The World's Columbian Exposition was a World's Fair held in Chicago in 1893 to celebrate the 400th anniversary of Christopher Columbus' arrival in the New World in 1492. The fair also intended to show the world that Chicago had risen from the ashes of the Great Fire in 1871. More than 27 million people attended the exposition during its six-month run from May 1st to October 30th.

TRAINED

CHAPTER 12.

WHEN CHICAGO WAS HOLLYWOOD: AT ONE TIME IN THE SILENT ERA, CHICAGO WAS THE FILM CAPITAL OF THE WORLD

1907-20

In January, 1915, Charlie Chaplin wandered miserably to work at Essanay Studios, the uptown film studio where he had recently been hired, and where he spent all day trying to find the boss, George Spoor, who still hadn't given him the large signing bonus he was promised. Chaplin, one of the nascent film industry's rising stars, had arrived in Chicago shortly before Christmas, 1914, and his arrival should have cemented Chicago's reputation as the motion picture capital of the world.

By January, Chaplin was starting to think it was the worst decision he had ever made. He had just left sunny California and arrived in Chicago during a week when the high temperature barely got above 20 degrees Fahrenheit. Even though he was making a huge salary, Chaplin was a notorious skinflint, sleeping on people's couches, borrowing coats, and buying a new "tramp" costume from a thrift store in the Loop, right near the theater at 11th and Wabash where he had made his Chicago debut with a Vaudeville troupe a few years before.

 Police was Chaplin's 14th film from Essanay, released in 1916

POLICE"

HERE'S THE LATEST

Essanay-Chaplin

FEATURE COMEDY

CHARLIE CHAPLIN himself says: *"It's a scream."*

You'll need to call out the reserves to hold the crowds when you book this newest laugh maker,

"POLICE"

It's a riot of fun; every foot packed with mirth.

RELEASED MAY 27

through all branches of the

GENERAL FILM CO.

Essanay

GEORGE K. SPOOR, PRESIDENT

1333 Argyle St., Chicago

When he arrived at the studio on his first day, Louella Parsons, who worked at the front desk, handed him a script.

"I don't use other people's scripts," Chaplin said. "I write my own."

He quickly devised a "scenario," then selected a leading lady from Essanay's cast of extras—a pretty young girl from the neighborhood. He spent an afternoon trying to teach her comedy and pratfalls, but she was a hopeless case. "I'm sorry, Mr. Chaplin," she said. "I just don't think any of this is funny."

Chaplin picked a new leading lady, but the young girl from the neighborhood's career recovered nicely. It was Gloria Swanson, whose fame would one day rival Chaplin's own. Although this time, for Chaplin's first film for Essanay, *His New Job*, Swanson ended up being relegated to the role of an extra.

Meanwhile, Francis X. Bushman, the biggest matinee idol of the day, tried to reassure Chaplin that it wasn't as bad as he thought. "Whatever you think of the studio," he said, "it's the antithesis."

"I don't like the studio," said Chaplin. "And I don't like the word 'antithesis.'"

He was only joking, but Essanay was not a good fit for Chaplin. He

Gloria Swanson, *Don't Change Your Husband*, 1919; and Francis X. Bushman, Charlie Chaplin and G.M. Anderson in *Broncho Billy*, 1915

only worked at their Chicago studio for a few weeks before transferring to their California lot, and George Spoor, the film pioneer who ran the studio, was unable to hold onto him when his contract expired. Throughout 1915 he became a bigger and bigger star, but when he returned to Chicago the next year as the biggest star in the world, he was working for another studio, and Chicago's reign as the film capital of the world was over.

But for much of the previous 20 years, when movies were truly in their infancy, Chicago had enjoyed a brief stint as the prototype for Hollywood. Chicago films included the first adventure serial, the first Sherlock Holmes movie, some of the first color films, and the first "mockumentaries," fictional films disguised as documentaries.

In fact, Chicago had been intended to be the birthplace of movies, the place where "moving pictures" would be introduced to the world. Thomas Edison's invention of the phonograph—a device which could record voices, so that the voices of famous people could be played and preserved long after their death—had made him famous. Sounds had always been as ephemeral as the wind, and the ability to record them and archive them was seen as nothing short of a miracle. It was so shocking that many magicians came to his lab, intent on proving that the device was a fake, and that Edison was merely a ventriloquist. In the late 1880s, he began to work on a device to make pictures move: the kinetoscope. The prototypes that his staff built were large boxes; people could put a coin into a slot, then peer into a hole about the size of a silver dollar, turn a crank, and see a moving picture show that lasted about a minute. He was teasing the press with descriptions of the device by 1890, and told people who visited his New Jersey lab that he intended to have a "kinetoscope pavillion" at the Columbian Exposition: the World's Fair that was being planned for Chicago.

The World's Fair of 1893 was like a preview of what the 20th century would be like. Attracting twenty-seven million paid admissions, the fair featured more than 200 buildings, each lined with brilliant electric light bulbs—gadgets that many fair patrons had never seen before. Among the fairgrounds, they could sample the phonograph recording machines they had been reading about for years, but had probably never

The cast and crew of Essanay Film Manufacturing Company, 1914

actually encountered, and watch Nikola Tesla conduct electric bolts right through his body. They could see early examples of a "horseless carriage" and an automatic dishwasher. They could sample new foods, such as hot dogs and hamburgers. And they could travel to the fair on Chicago's first elevated train line.

But one thing was missing: the kinetoscope. W.L. Dickson, the staffer that Edison had put in charge of the invention (he usually farmed out much of the actual inventing to his staff) suffered a nervous breakdown, and the device wasn't quite ready. Chicago wouldn't see one until a kinetoscope parlor opened downtown the next year, where people could thrill to such moving picture shows as "The Kiss," and "Seminary Girls," which may have been tame, but *was* a movie of Catholic school girls having pillow fights in their pajamas. Even the earliest filmmakers seemed to instinctively know what would sell.

There *were*, however, some moving pictures on display at the fair in 1893: there was a device called the tachyscope that was sort of a clumsy precursor to the kinetoscope, and Eduard "Eadweard" Muybridge, the man who is credited with having discovered the concept of "moving pictures" to begin with, was actually projecting moving images on the wall as part of the lectures on animal locomotion that he hosted in his "Zoopraxographical Hall," a midway attraction that was, in many ways, the first paid movie theater (it was a complete flop—given a choice between seeing a lecture on animal locomotion and the belly dancers nearby, practically everyone went with the belly dancers). Many early pioneers of the film industry saw these at the fair and were inspired by them.

Over the next several years, many advances in moving pictures would be made. Colonel William Selig would form the Selig Polyscope Company, a huge movie studio on the northwest side of Chicago. George Spoor would team up with a suburban inventor to form one of the first movie studios on the planet, and would go on to create *The Great Train Robbery,* which some pinpoint as the first real hit movie, before teaming up with "Broncho Billy" Anderson to form Essanay Studios on the north side of Chicago. Both men cited the things they had seen at the World's Fair as inspirations.

The first film known to be shot in Chicago was *Police Parade*, shot by the French moving picture company The Lumiere Brothers in 1896. The movie, which survives today, is simply a long shot of policemen walking by in parade formation. Of the several hundred policemen present in the film, only one of them doesn't sport a large mustache.

But in those early days, Thomas Edison was able to retake control of the movie business by securing patents to most movie-making equipment, so that no one could make or exhibit movies without paying him off. Chicago became a haven for movie-

Main building of Selig Polyscope Studio at 3900 North Claremont makers early on simply because it was far enough from Edison's east coast base to stay out of his radar.

By 1910, Essanay and Selig Polyscope were among the biggest movie studios on the planet, having eventually reached an agreement with Edison and forming a "trust" that kept competition low. Chicago's stature in the industry was so great that even the studios that were based in New York and elsewhere were obligated to have Chicago offices. Soon, the uptown neighborhood became a sort of prototype Beverly Hills, and the stars lived in luxury. Francis X. Bushman, the matinee idol, took to driving around in a purple limousine that had a special spotlight mounted on the dashboard so that people could see his famous profile as he drove past. Selig brought in a young man named Tom Mix to make cowboy movies, and hired Kathyln Williams, an actor-director who became one of the biggest stars of the day, to star in the *Adventures of Kathyln* serial, whose cross-promotions with the *Chicago Tribune* helped improve motion pictures' reputation as serious entertainment.

Perhaps the most innovative films of the era were the first Oz movies: a series of short silent moving pictures that L. Frank Baum, author of *The Wizard of Oz,* interacted with live onstage in a touring show that he called "The Fairylogue and Radio Plays." What he meant by "radio" is a mystery; the term "radio play" as a term for entertainment had never been used before, and wouldn't be again for several years.

The Adventures of Kathlyn, 1913; and 1910 silent film, *The Wonderful Wizard of Oz*

But a series of problems cost Chicago its reign as a film capital, not the least of which was that California not only offered a more varied terrain, it offered a climate far more suitable than the notoriously grey and cold Chicago. Selig was the first to open a studio in Hollywood, and in a very short time, Los Angeles went from a small town to an entire city that revolved around the motion picture industry. The last of the Chicago studios had closed their doors by 1920, and nearly all of the silent films shot in Chicago are now lost. But a new generation of scholars has discovered Chicago's contribution to early cinema, and author Andrew Erish recently published a biography of Selig entitled *The Man Who Invented Hollywood*

Essanay Studios' soundstage is now a part of St. Augustine College at 1345 West Argyle Street; a vault in the basement still says "SAFETY: FILM ONLY" on the door. Formal tours are not available, though staff are usually happy to show visitors around. Not far away, the old Selig Polyscope building stands at the corner of Byron and Claremont. Though the "greenhouse" studio that was once on the roof is long gone, and the building has long been converted into condos, Selig's trademark "Diamond S" logo is still visible above the front door, a subtle reminder of the days when Chicago was a major center of film production.

CHAPTER 13.

THE BLACK SOX SCANDAL: THE SHOCKING STORY THAT NEARLY DESTROYED BASEBALL

1919

It may be difficult to imagine now, but in the first few decades of the 20th century, Chicago's two teams, the Cubs and the White Sox, dominated Major League Baseball. Charles Comiskey, the owner of the Sox, said that Chicago was the best town for baseball. "Chicago is the greatest of all baseball cities," he proudly told G.W. Axelson, his biographer, around 1919. "I make no exception, though I have been treated well wherever I've been. It's the greatest city because the fans will stick to a loser season after season."

Comiskey could not have imagined just how prescient his statement would turn out to be. Nearly a century after he said it, the Chicago Cubs have not won a single World Series, and, though his own White Sox had just won in 1917, they would not win it again until 2005.

The Sox had just lost the 1919 Series when Comiskey made the statement. He had faith that the fans would stick with the team, but he did not realize at the time that the Sox had actually lost the Series on purpose. The Series had been "fixed," and the resulting scandal would almost destroy the nation's confidence in its most hallowed institution: baseball.

 Charles Comiskey, St. Louis Browns, baseball card portrait, 1887

COMISKEY - 1ST BASE ST. LOUIS.

Comiskey at the opening of his million-dollar ball park in 1910

Baseball may have had its origins in the English games of Rounders and Stool Ball, "stick and ball" games that go back to Shakespeare's day, but by Comiskey's day it had become a uniquely American institution. The game caught on in the middle of the 1800s in major cities such as Chicago and New York, and then spread around the country during the Civil War, when countless soldiers were introduced to the sport and played it every chance they got in their hundreds of circling camps. Soldiers who lived in the country brought the game home with them, and within a few years after the end of the war, writers were starting to refer to the game as America's "national pastime."

Born in 1859, Comiskey was a Chicagoan by birth, a member of a generation who grew up in the shadow of the rubble from the Great Chicago Fire of 1872, and in a world when baseball was a new and exciting American sport. He had taken up pitching after wandering into a game played in a vacant lot while he was supposed to be doing chores for his father, a local official known as "Honest John" Comiskey. By 1876, he was pitching for a Milwaukee team and making $50 a month, which was a pretty good salary at the time.

Gradually rising to become a manager, and eventually buying a team of his own, Comiskey's story was in many ways a uniquely American one. He became the first man to rise from being a player to being a team owner when he bought a St. Paul team in 1894, and eventually moved them to Chicago in 1900 under the name The White Stockings. Soon, they were playing in a sparkling field that bore Comiskey's name: Comiskey Park

Although he was one of baseball's first heroes, and though his team was a force to be reckoned with, Old Man Comiskey was widely hated by his players. He was notoriously stingy with them. "Shoeless Joe," his star player, made $6,000 a year; not exactly a paltry sum in those days, but less than a third of what the Detroit Tigers were paying Ty Cobb. There was no negotiating salaries with Comiskey, and no free agency clause in contracts, making his players little more than indentured servants. Money was deducted from the players' salaries to pay for laundering their uniforms, and their per diem payout for meals on away games was notably less than what other teams got. When they won the World Series in 1917, the payout of the prize money came to about $1500 a player (it should have been more), and the "bonus" he had promised them turned out not to be cash, as the players had believed it would be, but a case of flat, cheap champagne.

Things got worse during the 1919 season, as the White Sox battled fiercely for the pennant. Comiskey promised pitcher Eddie Cicotte a large bonus (some versions of the story say $10,000) if he won 30 games that year, and when he got as high as 28, Comiskey had him sidelined for the rest of the season. Comiskey said it was to rest him up for the World Series, but Cicotte suspected otherwise.

The players got their revenge.

They won the pennant, setting them up for a World Series contest against the Cincinnati Reds. Excitement for the series in Ohio was unusually high, as the Reds had never played in a World Series before, and hotel rooms became so scarce that a city ordinance was made allowing fans to sleep in the city parks.

Crowds gathered to hear the reporting for Game 3 of the 1919 World Series. October 3, 1919

In one hotel, though, eight members of the White Sox were taking meetings with gamblers who offered the men $100,000 if they lost the Series. Even divided eight ways, this was far more than they were getting

Shoeless Joe Jackson

from Comiskey if they won.

People still argue about who was really in on the fix and whether the Sox fixed the Series at all. Shoeless Joe Jackson apparently wanted no part of it, and even asked Comiskey to sit him out of the first game so he didn't get his hands dirty (Comiskey may well have heard rumors that a fix was in the works). Some say that the Sox certainly lost the first game on purpose (they lost 9 to 1), but when the gamblers didn't pay up as expected, they proceeded to fight their level best for the rest of the Series and lost it fair and square.

By September of the next year, rumors about the fix had gotten so loud that a grand jury was called to investigate the story. It was Cicotte who broke the news to Comiskey that the rumors were true. "I have played a crooked game," he said, perhaps with a bit of triumph remembering how he had been cheated out of a bonus, "and I have lost."

Comiskey immediately suspended several players accused in the fix, probably costing his team the 1920 pennant by benching some of the best men. The trial dragged in to 1921, and, though no players were ever convicted on criminal charges, eight of them were banned from the sport for life, including Shoeless Joe, and baseball's reputation may have never fully recovered. Chicago Fans would forever refer to the 1919 team as "The Black Sox." Comiskey himself remained involved in baseball until his death; he was inducted into the Hall of Fame in 1939, but it is possible that his name became a curse on the team. The White Sox would not win another World Series until 2005, the year that the newly rebuilt stadium's name was changed from New Comiskey Park to U.S. Cellular Field.

U.S. Cellular Field stands right near the original site of Comiskey Park, near the “Sox 35th” red line El stop. Locals seldom say “U.S. Cellular Field;” most prefer simply saying “Sox Park.” A trip north on the red line to the Addison stop will take you right to Wrigley Field, where the Cubs play.

SHOELESS JOE

It's hard to argue that "Shoeless Joe" Jackson, the star of the team, was playing to lose; he batted .375 in the World Series and hit the only home run of the series. Many players later said that Jackson was never truly involved. But the ban sticks, and he is still not in the Hall of Fame.

In 1999, the U.S. House of Representatives passed a resolution urging Major League Baseball to reconsider Jackson's guilt and ban. The case is still considered "under review" as of 2013.

1919 Chicago Black Sox

CHAPTER 14.

MARGARET SEITHAMIER'S REVENGE: THE CRIMES THAT INSPIRED THE MUSICAL *CHICAGO*

1919

In July, 1919, 16-year-old Margaret Seithamier sat with her half-sister, Marie Hermes in a prison cell. The two were laughing and singing when a reporter came in to speak with them.

"Say," said Margaret. "Did that guy I shot today die? I hope he did."

"If Marge hadn't done it," Marie added, "I'd've shot him myself. He needed it."

Margaret kept laughing as she described the scene to the *Tribune* reporter of when the police first took her into the station. "A blonde came in and asked to see who shot Benny Burr. They pointed me out to her . . . and then she keeled right over and fainted. That was the blonde he told me he was going to marry. Believe me, she looked cheesy! She looked like one of these little seamstresses with a black cap on her head who sews for a living. You would think a lawyer who thought he was somebody could pick out something classier than that. He told me he spent money on this blonde and gave her a swell education. Huh. And

120 Chicago (1927), Phyllis Haver portrayed on the movie poster

CHICAGO
CITY
ROXIE

Phyllis Haver as Roxie Hart, *Chicago*, 1927 and; "Poison Widow" Tillie Klimek, 1923

what she looks like! Say, matron, ain't we gonna have no looking glass at all? And say, those were rotten sandwiches. There's mine over in the corner."

One could not exactly call Margaret Seithamier a fine and charming young woman. But wheels were already in motion to portray her as one in court.

In the hit musical *Chicago*, showgirl Roxie Hart kills her lover, then hires a lawyer who tries to portray her in court as a sympathetic ingenue who never meant to kill the poor man. Though the story in the musical was fiction, this sort of technique was well known in the Chicago criminal courts—and very successful, too. Women were brought to trial for murder in Chicago many times, but they were hardly ever convicted, and not a single woman was ever hanged in Cook County. Chicago lawyers in those days were experts in making the jury sympathize with women—especially if they were pretty. In the early part of the 20th century, seven out of nine women brought to trial for murder in Cook County were acquitted.

Reporters who knew this had a field day when Tillie Klimek, an unattractive woman, was brought to trial for poisoning one of her husbands (one of at least four she was thought to have poisoned, along with various relatives and neighbors). Her cousin Nellie, who was accused along with her, was equally dowdy. "They are," wrote crime reporter Genevieve Forbes Herrick, "without guile or the aid of hairdresser . . . they carry no vanity box, rouge or lipstick. The upturned brims of their plain black hats are uncompromising and refuse to cast kind shadows over their faces. They don't bite their lips when in distress." In a later article, after Tillie was found guilty, Herrick wrote "No jugglery of words could bring her into the sorority of ladies, beauteous or wistful or bashing, who could pull the trigger and smile their way out . . . it was the lack of white powder on her nose more than the presence of white powder on the meat (arsenic) that sent her behind bars."

Margaret Seithamier wasn't the world's most sympathetic character, either. She looked at least five years older than she was, and had been a ward of the state since her early teens. She had been arrested before in the company of "rough" boys who had raps for hold-ups, and she was ignoring the state's orders by working in a hotel.

The man she shot, attorney Benjamin Burr, was not a well-respected character; he was known as a sneaky, two-timing liar, not to mention a statutory rapist. Margaret had met him during her mother's divorce proceedings; he began taking her out to cabarets and hotels for drinks, and she often spent the night at his house. Not willing to be cast aside, when he began to lose interest in her she confronted him in his office and shot him to death.

Marie Hermes and Margaret Seithamier guarded by a policeman, 1919

The tangled drama fascinated the press. All the while when he was involved with Margaret, Burr had also been carrying on

Roxie Hart, 1942: Ginger Rogers and Adolphe Menjou

with the "blonde" that he planned to marry, as well as with a common-law wife with whom he had a child. He was also apparently going after Marie, Margaret's half-sister, which was what made Margaret decide to get revenge with the aid of a firearm.

Burr's common-law wife reacted calmly to the news that he had been shot, and his seven-year-old daughter, Lucille, simply said "Is Daddy dead? Wasn't he nice, Ma, to give me a dollar when I went to the barber shop with him last Sunday?" Burr's mother, who had lived with him, sat cheerfully and said that none of what happened mattered to her, because she would be dead soon, anyway.

Margaret had also threatened to shoot the blonde. She threatened to shoot lots of people.

"She observed," wrote the *Tribune,* "that juries are chivalrous in Cook County and that women are never hanged. So she came to the conclusion that it was open season all the time and went out and killed her man."

She was certainly operating under a belief that she couldn't be hanged as a minor; she even told the jury at her inquest that she had gone to another attorney who told her that this was the case, and that she might as well go out and shoot him. Her own attorney, W.W. O'Brien, also pushed the case that a juvenile couldn't be hanged. The state's attorney, though, said that a criminal could be hanged at 14, if the jury decided it. "According to common law, ten years is the minimum age," Judge Dennis Sullivan chimed in. "But you know juries."

Another judge present, Charles Foell, said "Seven's enough, but I don't think it's been done recently."

O'Brien had coached Margaret, and at the inquest her attorney announced that her *real* motive for killing Burr was that he had impregnated her, not merely scorned her.

"Why didn't Margaret mention this before?" O'Brien was asked. "Why did she tell the police that she killed him just because she was jealous?"

"Ah," O'Brien said. "Women are sensitive about those things."

The version of events he presented at the inquest tried to paint Margaret in a flattering light. She was, he said, "a simple, trusting girl. She loved Burr—loved him with that intensity of passion that knows no law. He told her her affection was returned. She looked up to the attorney and loved him with childlike devotion. What happens? Insidiously, Burr introduced her to cabarets and cocktails. One morning she awoke in his apartment. She wept bitterly, but he consoled her and assured her that he loved her. He bought her clothes. One day, with her heart fluttering, she visited his office. Paling and blushing by turns, she told him her secret. He laughed sardonically. Taking the picture of a beautiful blonde girl from his desk, he showed it to her and said, 'There's the girl I'm going to marry.' Broken-hearted, she killed him."

On the stand at the trial three months later, Margaret told this story in her sweetest voice, with what the *Tribune* called "an affected lisp—(she) recited her story in a singsong manner as if she were reciting a lesson in a schoolroom." She would have been nearly unrecognizable to people who had seen her as she sat laughing in the police station only three months before about how she had shot Benny Burr . By now, though, the story had necessarily changed a bit, as it was obvious that Margaret was not pregnant. Now, the story was that Margaret had *thought* she was pregnant.

In cross-examination, she told how she had first gone to Burr's apartment on January 29, 1919—her sixteenth birthday—where she had drinks and stayed the night. The next morning, she said, Benny

Chicago Criminal Courts Building, 1964

announced his intention to marry her.

But seven months later, she said, she called him on the telephone. "I told him I thought I was in a delicate condition," she said, "and I asked him if he was going to marry me. I told him if he didn't marry me I was going to kill myself and he could hear the shot over the telephone."

Instead, though, according to the new version of the story, she took a gun to his office to kill herself right in front of him. He had fought to take the gun from her, and the gun had discharged in the struggle. The fact that it hit Benny Burr was all an accident.

The next day, the jury acquitted her of the murder of Benjamin Burr. She was not exactly set free, though, as the judge ordered her to a school for girls known as The House of the Good Shepherd. There, a month later, she started a riot in which she and several other girls beat up a nun in an attempt to escape.

After that, though, she became a model prisoner, and a year later she was released into her mother's custody. She had learned typing and accounting and took a job in an office on West Thirty-Fifth Street. The story of Margaret Seithamier faded from public memory fairly quickly, buried among many similar stories that played out in the old courthouse building that still stands at Hubbard and Dearborn Streets, right behind the fire station that marks the site of the old jail and the gallows Margaret knew she would never see. The courthouse building houses offices today, but the lobby displays portraits of several people—all men—who were brought to trial within its walls.

MAURINE WATKINS AND *CHICAGO*

Maurine D. Watkins

The crimes, corruption, and "celebrity" criminals in Prohibition-era Chicago have inspired plays, films, and the infamous Tony Award-wining Chicago, Broadway's longest running musical revival and the longest running American musical in Broadway history. The musical is based on the 1926 play by reporter Maurine Dallas Watkins, which grew out of the newspaper columns she wrote while assigned to a 1924 murder case. Her columns proved to be a big hit. The press and public were fascinated by homicides committed by women, often young and pretty, who were accused of killing their husbands or lovers, but always seemed to be acquitted by all-male juries.

The Broadway show, choreographed by Bob Fosse, with music by John Kander and lyrics by Fred Ebb, has also toured nationally and internationally, and inspired the Academy Award-winning 2002 film starring Renee Zellweger, Catherine Zeta-Jones, Richard Gere, John C. Reilly, and Queen Latifah.

CHICAGO CRIMINAL COURT

The courthouse where Margaret Seithamier was tried is an office building now on the corner of Hubbard and Dearborn streets. The lobby is decorated with portraits of famous people who were tried in the building, including Terrible Tommy O'Connor, who escaped and was never caught. The city stopped hanging convicts in 1927, but had to keep the gallows in storage for decades in case O'Connor was caught, since he had been sentenced to hang.

CHAPTER 15.

LILLIAN COLLIER AND THE SNUGGLEPUPPIES: A YOUNG FLAPPER'S CRUSADE TO BRING HIGH ART TO CHICAGO

1922

"There is no snugglepupping at the Wind Blew Inn."

So said Miss Lillian Collier, the young proprietress of the Wind Blew Inn, a bohemian tea room on Michigan Avenue, as she stood on the stand in a courtroom in 1922. Her place had been raided due to concerns that she was hosting "petting parties" where "snugglepuppies" petted with "snugglepups" to the tune of syncopated "blues" music—in addition to serving liquor disguised as tea.

Born, supposedly, to New York circus performers around the turn of the 20th century, Miss Collier first made national attention when, in 1920, she was photographed spending a day trying out life as a steel worker perched atop a high building as part of a story she was researching as a reporter for a Chicago newspaper. Shortly thereafter, she thrilled a crowd by climbing up a flagpole amid high winds to hang up a pennant for the upcoming Pageant of Progress fair.

This was a few years before "flagpole sitting" became one of the oddest

---

 Women in Chicago being arrested for wearing one-piece bathing-suits, without the required leg coverings. 1922

Lillian Collier (right)

fads of the 1920s, but Lillian seems to have been a regular cultural vanguard in those days; she was part of the burgeoning "flapper" movement, and, by 1922, was one of the most notable bohemians in Chicago. Not quite 20 years old by most reports, she became the darling of the poets and artists who congregated at the Dil Pickle Club, the indoor open forum that operated near Bughouse Square and provided the soapbox orators with a place to hold court when the weather was too cold to draw an audience outdoors.

In late 1921, she opened her own "tea room"—the Wind Blew Inn—on Michigan Avenue, where the neighbors complained about the "syncopated blues" music that was heard through the windows. Rumors flew that she was hosting wild "petting parties" in the place, where young people engaged in "snugglepupping." The fact that she was prominently displaying Greek nude statues didn't help.

Early in 1922, the police raided the place, and newspapers around the country jumped at the chance to say that "the cops blew in to the Wind Blew Inn." Everyone present was arrested and hauled into court.

While she awaited trial, Miss Collier covered up the statues with overalls and granted an interview for a newspaper article that was syndicated in papers throughout the country. In the interview, she claimed that she had come to Chicago to "preach the gospel of real life" and convert heathens and "hicks" to "art."

She received the reporter in sandals and bare legs beneath her skirt—she wore no stockings, which was shocking at the time. Her bobbed hair was mentioned by every reporter who met her.

"Oh, art, where art thou?" she wailed as she showed off the overall-clad statues. "Bohemianism will come to Chicago, but it will take years, perhaps ages, maybe eons. Who knows? But I am willing to sacrifice myself to bring it a step nearer. You ask what is wrong with Chicago. This is it: too many folks just in from the corn belt. Really, they drive cows to pasture by here every morning. You know there aren't many real people here. I mean those who do the big things; those who see the light. But I'll try to struggle on and teach these people the value of aesthetic effectiveness."

On trial the next month, she and her partner, Virginia Harrison, swore that the strongest thing served at the Wind Blew Inn was chocolate eclairs (which regulars claimed decades later was not exactly true; the tea was spiked), and that "there is no snugglepupping at the Wind Blew Inn."

Speaking against her were police officers who testified that they'd seen couples, lit only by candles and surrounded by "weird art," cuddling and holding hands in the notorious den of sin and iniquity. The proprietor of the rooming house next door said he had lost patrons because no one could stand the bluesy piano music heard from the Inn at all hours.

A student named L. Franklin spoke in Collier's defense. "I heard that people of the 'genius' type went there," he said. "I wanted to see what they looked like." He was joined in testifying to the integrity of the place by Miss Collier's mother.

A woman dressed in flapper fashion delivers a speech from atop a soapbox

Judge Jacobs dismissed all of those arrested for "snugglepupping," but continued the case of Collier herself for the next month.

The next month, she was either behaving herself or making

a good show of doing so. When Reverend John Williamson, Mayor Thompson's cabinet officer, came in to try to buy bootleg liquor, he ordered Russian tea and lemon cream pie, then asked for booze.

Collier, the paper said, "Shook her pretty bobbed hair."
"No, we run a strictly decent place," she said. "We never have anything like that here."

Reverend Williamson didn't believe it, but he left the place thirsty. Collier was nothing if not shrewd.

At her trial weeks later, the exchanges between Lillian, Virginia and the judge should probably have become legendary.

"We are merely trying to live life as we see it," the papers quoted Collier as saying. Next to her, Virginia Harrison, then described in papers as her "aide" (later commentators have assumed she was her girlfriend) nodded her assent.

"Have either of you ever read *Little Women*, *Flaxie Frizzie*, or Hans Christian Anderson's tales?" asked the judge.

The two shook their heads. "But we read bed-time stories in the papers," Lillian offered.

"Well, that's good," said the judge. "All that's the matter with you is that you have a false value of the things of life in general. Start on the fairy tales right away."

And so the two were sentenced to read a book of fairy tales to cure their bohemian ideals.

Lillian and Virginia dutifully marched to the library and checked out just such a book, telling reporters that they promised to stop promoting bohemianism if the stories worked as advertised.

Of course, they didn't, and Collier kept on running the tea house. But a month later, the Wind Blew Inn burned down. The result, Collier said, of "puritan arsonists." A new location was opened on LaSalle, but it was cleaner, and, therefore, less successful. Years later, a regular noted that "people wanted some dirt with their seventy-five-cent tea." Lillian's days as a tea room proprietress might have come to an end that day, but she continued to make the news. Two years later, a widely circulated article entitled "Is Today's Girl Becoming a Savage?" appeared in several newspapers and featured Lillian prominently. Here, she defended the "modern girl" and comes off as a sort of 1920s prototype of later feminists.

Lady Frances Balfour

Lady Balfour, a prominent member of the British aristocratic wing of suffragists, had slammed the flapper movement as women did "everything to imitate the courtesan. Her face is a mass of powder. Her lips are gashed out of human resemblance. And a reek of her in passing makes one long for a breath off the heather."

"Lady Balfour had best know the flapper before she condemns her," Collier told a reporter in reply. "Women too long have played the role of the underdog. That's why they have been tread upon since the days of the cave man. Relegated to menial work, it was with fear and trembling that they came to the lords and masters. Now woman has broken the traditional bond. She has emerged from restraint that made the old-time demure miss, who was a demure miss simply because she dared not be otherwise. The woman of yesterday was a box of suppressed desires. Timidity was her watchword, coquetry another name for hoaxing folks. The flapper of today typifies understanding. She is the product of a new age turning toward the light . . . regardless of what Lady Balfour says, the flapper will survive. She is in the process of still further evolution, and since evolution tends ever upward, turn the light on your fears and don't worry."

After this remarkable interview, Miss Collier's life has proved

Flappers dancing the Charleston atop the Sherman Hotel, 1926

impossible to trace—she may have drifted back to New York and opened another version of the Wind Blew Inn that opened and closed without a fuss. Several women named Lillian Collier have been uncovered: a suffragist in Texas, a poet in Canada, a New York socialite who married an Olympic fencer—who was killed in a Zeppelin crash shortly after the wedding. None, however, seem to be the same Lillian Collier whose antics took Chicago by storm. Whatever became of her has become another classic unsolved Chicago mystery.

But one thing is for sure: she would be thrilled with the way that Chicago grew. Though the area around North Michigan Avenue and the Water Tower are no longer the bohemian enclaves they were in her day, it is hard not to imagine that she would be pleased by the number of galleries and bohemian enclaves that have sprung up around the city in the decades following her era. She would love the galleries on Fulton Market Street, the road extending west of the Loop where art galleries sit side by side with meat packing plants. Art has come to Chicago at last.

TOWERTOWN

In 1920, when Lillian Collier opened her tea room, it was not yet uncommon to see cows on North Michigan Avenue. They surrounded "Towertown," an area that was known as an artsy enclave.

OLD CHICAGO SCENE: Oak Street beach, c. 1925

CHAPTER 16.

THE SAINT VALENTINE'S DAY MASSACRE: THE MOST FAMOUS EVENT IN CHICAGO GANGLAND HISTORY

1929

"They're full of dead men in there!"

Valentine's Day, 1929. A man in a Clark Street rooming house was sent across the street by his landlady to see what was going on at the SMC Cartage Company, a quiet little garage where she had just heard a loud disturbance. She had seen a police car pull up, then drive away minutes later after some loud commotion. A dog was barking on the inside.

When the man stuck his head in, he saw seven men lying in pools of blood. A soft voice said "Who's there?"

He had just discovered the aftermath of the St. Valentine's Day Massacre, the most notorious event in Chicago gangland history.

When the police and ambulances arrived, they were able to piece together a bit of what had happened. A stolen police car full of gangsters in cop uniforms had come into the garage and lined seven men up against the wall. Presumably, the men in the cop uniforms were

A crowd stands in front of the SMC Cartage Co. garage on North Clark on Feb. 14, 1929 following the St. Valentine's Day massacre

looking for the gangsters' boss, George "Bugs" Moran, who had become the head of the north side mob after all the smarter, more-capable leaders had been bumped off over the previous four years. Perhaps, upon lining them up, someone had shouted "Which one of you mugs is Bugs Moran?"

But none of them *was* Moran, so no one said anything. In response, the shooters pulled out Thompson submachine guns and shot all seven of them.

Six were probably dead before they hit the ground.

The one man who had said "Who's there" when the scene was discovered was Frank Gusenberg, one of the most notorious hit men of the north side. His brother, Pete, lay dead along the wall.

The police officers naturally recognized Gusenberg—they knew most of the major gangsters by sight—and followed the ambulance to the hospital. His wounds were judged to be fatal, but doctors were able to stabilize him enough that he could talk a little."Frank," said the cops, "you're going to die. You've got to tell us who did this to you before you go. Who shot you?"

But Gusenberg was a gangster, and gangsters didn't squawk. No matter what happened. And even in this "tell no tales" world, Frank was known as "Tight Lips Gusenberg."

With his fading breath, Gusenberg looked up at the police, and perhaps even managed a weak, rueful smile as he said "Nobody shot me."

Moments later, he died of having been shot several times. There were more than a dozen bullet wounds in his body.

The rest of the men in the garage had soon been identified. In all, five of them were notable gangsters from the north side. Another, John May, was an ex-gangster who had been hired to do some maintenance work on the gangsters' trucks. He had been trying to get out of the gang world, but needed the money to feed his family.

The other man was Reinhardt Schwimmer, a 27-year-old retired (or possibly failed) optometrist who was living off his mother-in-law. He wasn't a member of the gang, just a young man who thought it was cool to hang out with gangsters. He enjoyed bragging to his non-gang friends that he could have people killed if he wanted to.

If anyone thought he had no brains in his head, they only had to look at the photos the next day, which showed his brains sitting next to his hat.

Moran himself had been planning to meet up with his gang at the garage that day; apparently a big shipment of bootleg liquor was coming in. But he had arrived late and, seeing the stolen police squad car parked outside, assumed that there was a liquor raid going on. Rather than get arrested (or, as it turned out, shot to death), he ducked into a nearby coffee shop and had what must have been the best cup of coffee of his life.

When asked if he knew what had happened, Moran is reputed to have said what everyone in town was thinking: "The only person who kills guys like that is Al Capone."

Indeed, no one seemed to doubt that Capone and his men, the chief rivals of the north side mob, were behind the massacre. The police quickly arrested "Machine Gun" Jack McGurn, the Capone gang's best shooter, and John Scalise and Albert Anselmi, two hit men that Capone had employed before. The two men were both ruthless and pretty much brainless—two of the main qualities the shooters must have possessed. Shooting seven men, but not the guy they were supposed to be shooting, was exactly the kind of stunt they might have played.

However, none of the charges the police had could ever stick. McGurn had a "blonde alibi"—he had been shut up in a hotel room with a showgirl the entire time.

And Capone's alibi was even better: he wasn't even in Chicago. He was in his compound in Miami, where he was spending most of his time by 1929. Fewer people there wanted to kill him than in Chicago, after all. At the moment when the massacre took place, he had been meeting with a state's attorney to discuss a recent mob hit in New York, an airtight alibi if there ever was one.

As the Chicago police cast a wide net over the city, gangsters began to find it convenient to go visit Capone. The prices of hotels in Miami doubled, then tripled as the gangsters came by the score, explaining to the reporters that though Miami was undoubtedly warmer than Chicago in February, there was "a lot of heat" in Chicago. One newspaper estimated that five hundred gangsters had left Chicago for Miami to wait for things to cool down.

The police found the burning wreck of the stolen police car used by the shooters in a west side garage, and with the find came a few bits of evidence connecting the shooting to The Circus Gang, a west side operation that was connected to Capone. However, there were never any convictions.

Scene from the Film *The St. Valentine's Day Massacre*, 1967; and George "Bugs" Moran

Today, the shooting remains a mystery. Every few months a new theory will go around; in the 1930s, tabloids and true crime magazines published an alleged "confession" from a man who said that Capone had brought in some out-of-town gangsters for the hit. They had set up camp in a rooming house across from the garage and seen a man they thought was Moran walking into the garage, then called in the hit to the Circus Cafe, the main hangout of the Circus Gang, just a couple of miles away from the Moran strongholds on the north side.

In recent years, a theory has gone around that Capone had nothing to do with the massacre at all, just as he always said. In this version of events, the man behind the hit was a gangster named "Three Fingered Jack" who had a vendetta against the Gusenberg brothers, who had killed his cousin some months before. The cousin's father was a cop, and perhaps he was the man who had provided the police car and uniforms for the massacre. This would explain why the police had never publicly cracked the case—they would have been implicating one of their own. However, there is a major flaw in that theory: Three Fingered Jack was in jail the whole time.

One clue as to what happened may have been the fate of John Scalise and Albert Anselmi: in May of 1929, just a few months after the massacre, their bodies were found beside the road in Indiana, having been beaten to bloody pulps with baseball bats and shot in the head.

Al Capone's cell as it exists today at Eastern State Penitentiary

The "official" version of their death holds that Capone had found out that they were plotting to kill him and take over the gang, some speculate that their murder could have been Capone's revenge for bungling the St. Valentine's job so badly, failing to hit their actual target and bringing untold amounts of heat onto the gang.

Capone certainly seemed to be fearing for his life. He hastily organized a "peace conference" in Atlantic City, attended by most of the major players in the gang world, allegedly including not only his old boss, John Torrio, but his chief rival, Bugs Moran himself. What went on at this peace conference isn't exactly known, but Capone seems to have left it fearing for his life: just after the conference, he went to Philadelphia, where he was almost immediately arrested for weapons possession by a cop who was actually a friend of his. He quickly pleaded guilty and spent the next year in the relative safety of a well-appointed Pennsylvania prison cell, where by most accounts he was treated more like a guest than a prisoner.

By the time of his release, Chicago was a changed place. The massacre had finally spurred the federal government to get involved in the fight against the underworld and the bootleggers, and Capone couldn't control the Feds the way he could control the local police. He was eventually convicted of tax evasion charges and ended up spending several years in Alcatraz, emerging as a shell of the man he had once been, his brain ravaged by syphilis. He would never again enjoy anything like the power he had enjoyed the day before the massacre.

The SMC Cartage Company garage at 2120 North Clark Street remained standing for nearly forty years, hosting a series of different businesses that seemed to attract more curiosity seekers than customers. Bullet holes could still be seen in the north wall, where the men were lined up. It was torn down in the late 1960s, and today bricks said to be from the building command as much as $1,500 on the collectors' market. Only a field and parking area mark the spot today; a senior apartment complex, which some residents say is haunted, sits next door. Across the street sits the famous Chicago Pizza and Oven Grinder restaurant, which some say was the place where the lookouts were stationed. A tree in the middle of the field marked the spot where the north wall would have been until 2013, when it was cut down. No plaque or marker signifies the historic spot at all.

AFTER THE MASSACRE

The massacre was the beginning of the end for Capone. After that, the feds were finally motivated to get involved, and he was convicted of tax evasion in 1931. By the time he got out of prison, his brain had been destroyed by syhphilis, and the gang went on without him.

NOT ONLY CAPONE

Although everyone in the world who hears where Chicagoans come from will say, "Al Capone!, bang bang!", there were other celebrity criminals in Chicago.

H.H. Holms (1861-1896)

Born in 1861 in Gilmanton, New Hampshire, H.H. Holmes was one of America's first serial killers. In 1886, he moved to Chicago and took over a pharmacy in South Side Englewood. Then he built a three-story "Murder Castle" hotel, which housed many bizarre features—doors that led to nothing, rooms without windows, trapdoors and hidden passageways, and he lured numerous victims in during the 1893 Columbian Exposition. Once admitting to killing 27 people, estimates range from 20 to 100 victims, with some reports going as high as 200 victims. He was captured and hanged in 1896 in Philadelphia.

H.H. Holmes and "Murder Castle" in Englewood

John Dillinger (1903-1934)

John Herbert Dillinger was born in 1903 in Indianapolis. He was a bank robber during the Great Depression. His gang robbed two dozen banks and four police stations. Dillinger escaped from jail twice but was never convicted of the murder of an East Chicago police officer who shot at him, prompting him to return fire. It was Dillinger's only homicide charge. On his 31st birthday, June 22, 1934, Dillinger was declared America's first Public Enemy Number One. To go into hiding, Dillinger moved into Anna Sage's apartment in July, 1934. Originally from Romania, she was facing deportation proceedings for operating several brothels. Sage was working a double game. On July 22, 1934, Dillinger invited Sage and his girlfriend, Polly Hamilton, to see the Clark Gable movie *Manhattan Melodrama* at the Biograph Theatre near Lincoln Park. Sage had forewarned the FBI and, on that hot night, the trio went to see the film, while FBI agents waited outside. After the film they noticed Dillinger began to run, reaching into his pants pocket to draw a gun. He entered an alley just as a volley of gunfire greeted him. Four bullets hit Dillinger's body.

Anna Sage and the Biograph Theatre in 1934

CHAPTER 17.

RESURRECTION MARY: CHICAGO'S MOST FAMOUS GHOST–THE VANISHING HITCHHIKER OF ARCHER AVENUE

1930s

When Brian saw the girl in the white dress sitting by the side of Archer Avenue, he thought it was a girl he knew from his high school. She was crying, and clearly needed help.

He pulled over beside her and rolled down the window. "You want a ride?"

When the girl looked up, he saw that it wasn't the girl he had thought it was, but a stranger, a pale blonde he had never seen before. But he couldn't very well drive away after offering her help. It would be rude.

Without a word, the girl in white stepped up from the curb and let herself into the passenger side of Brian's car. "Just take me up Archer, please," she said.

Brian proceeded up Archer, and tried to strike up a conversation, but the girl didn't seem to want to talk. All she would say was "the snows came early this year." She looked out the window, then out of the front

S.P
DŁUSKI

Archer Avenue

windshield, then over at Brian, then out the windshield again. Brian began to wonder if he had picked up a crazy person, or a girl with a drug problem.

Then she spoke up. “Pull over up here. Right here. Ahead,” she said.

“Up there?” he asked. “I’m not sure if I can. That’s the cemetery.”

“No!” she said, suddenly hysterical. “You *have* to. Pull over right now. Now!”

Confused, Brian pulled over towards the gates of Resurrection Cemetery, the largest of the many graveyards that dotted the southwest side along Archer Avenue, the old Indian trail that had been among the city’s earliest major arteries.

“All right,” he said. “Do you want me to walk you the rest of the way home?”

"No," she said. "Where I'm going, you can't follow me."

He looked up at the gates of the cemetery before him, then looked back at his passenger side. But the girl was gone. The window was still closed, and the door had never opened; the girl had simply disappeared.

He had just given a ride to Resurrection Mary, Chicago's most famous ghost.

The "Vanishing Hitchhiker" is a pretty standard urban legend. Variations on the story turn up all over the world, and have been going around since long before there were any automobiles from which they could hitch rides; there's even a variation on the story in the Bible. "Mary" isn't even the only ghost in Chicago; another young woman dressed in a 1920s "flapper" outfit hitches rides along Harlem and disappears into Waldheim Cemetery in suburban Forest Park. Another, younger woman is said to appear and disappear on a south side bus.

But one thing that most vanishing hitchers have in common is that it's impossible to track down a first-hand source; the story is usually something that happened to a friend of a friend of a friend of your cousin's roommate.

Mary differs in a couple of key ways: one is that researchers actually have *several* first-hand accounts of encounters with her dating back to the early 1930s.

Another is that vanishing hitchhiker stories usually feature several distinct characteristics: the girl is usually met at some place of entertainment, such as a dance hall. And the driver usually goes to her address after she vanishes, where her mother says "that couldn't have been my daughter; she died in a horrible car accident three years ago," at which point the baffled driver recognizes a photograph of his passenger on the wall inside. Often, he finds some outerwear he loaned the girl on her grave the next day.

When people in Chicago tell the story of Resurrection Mary, they usually include these motifs, but when one studies the actual first-hand accounts, most of them are absent. She's usually picked up (often by cab drivers) right by the side of the road, and seldom says anything in the car, other than asking the driver to drive up Archer Avenue. Only one man ever claimed to go to her house, and by the time he found the courage to share his story, he had forgotten the address.

If she said more, or if the man's memory served him better, we might be able to solve the enduring mystery of who, exactly, our beloved vanishing hitcher is the ghost of. Though some folklorists outright reject any attempt to connect a ghost like Mary to any actual girl, ghost hunters in Chicago have scoured the newspaper archives and death index trying to find out who the mysterious girl might be.

One popular candidate is Mary Bregovy, a beautiful 21-year-old girl who met a couple of boys at the Goldblatt Brothers' department store in March, 1934. Her friend thought they seemed too "wild," but when they offered to take her out drinking and dancing, Mary accepted. Over the course of the evening, they journeyed up to the Loop area, possibly after already having a few drinks, and wound up crashing the vehicle into the El track support beam at Wacker and Lake. Most of the passengers were fine, but Mary Bregovy was thrown through the windshield of the car and killed; she was pronounced dead on arrival at Iroquois Hospital, which stood only blocks away. Days later, she was buried in an unmarked grave at Resurrection Cemetery in an orchid-colored dress.

Since she was ballroom-hopping on the night of her death, connecting her to the usual legend in which vanishing hitchers are met at dance halls, she has emerged as one of the most popular candidates for the true identity of the famous ghost. However, some ghost hunters are not convinced. Most sightings indicate that the ghost is that of a blonde woman, and the surviving photographs of Mary Bregovy clearly show her as a beautiful brunette. Furthermore, there's some strong evidence that the story of a vanishing hitchhiker on Archer Avenue had already been going around for a few years by the time of her death in 1934.

Another recently popular candidate is Mary Miskowski, a resident of the south side "Back of the Yards" neighborhood who was 19 years old in 1930, when she is said to have been killed in a terrible car wreck on Archer Avenue on Halloween night, en route to a costume party and wearing her mother's old wedding dress. She would be a perfect candidate if the story were true; however, recent research has indicated that the terrible car wreck in question never happened; Ms. Miskowski actually died in the 1950s, by which time she was well older than the ghost so many people have encountered.

There are at least sixty young women named Mary who were buried at Resurrection Cemetery between 1915 and 1935. And to assume that the ghost is one of them is making the broad assumption that "Mary" is actually the ghost's name in the first place; people who meet the ghost rarely get her to say much, and she never seems to mention her name. It could be that we simply call her Resurrection Mary because it has a better ring to it than "Resurrection Beulah."

Whoever she is, Resurrection Mary has captured the imagination of several generations of Chicagoans, and cruising up and down Archer Avenue looking for the elusive ghost has long been a rite of passage for teenagers. Over the years, she has emerged as the most famous of all vanishing hitchhikers.

Resurrection Cemetery is located in the suburb of Justice at 7200 South Archer Avenue. Richard T. Crowe, who helped transform Mary from a local legend to an international celebrity during his career as Chicago's first full-time professional ghost hunter, was buried there in 2012.

CHAPTER 18.

THE CURSE OF THE CUBS: IS THE CUBS' LONG LOSING STREAK REALLY BECAUSE OF A GOAT?

1945

In the early 1980s, Steve Goodman wrote perhaps his most enduring song, "The Dying Cub Fan's Last Request." Among the many pithy lines in the song was this gem: "You know the law of averages? They say anything will happen that can. But the last time the Cubs won a National League Pennant was the year we dropped the bomb on Japan."

More than 30 years—and 30 seasons—later, the line is still true. The Chicago Cubs have not played in the World Series since 1945, and they haven't *won* it since 1907. Time and again they have made the playoffs, only to be shut out of the Series itself.

And some people blame it all on a goat.

In October, 1945, the Cubs were battling the Detroit Tigers in the World Series, and were leading two games to one when they played an afternoon game at Wrigley Field (all games were day games then; Wrigley Field, a gloriously old-fashioned ballpark, wouldn't get lights until the late 1980s). Billy Sianis, the proprietor of the Billy Goat Tavern

 A program from the 1945 World Series between the Detroit Tigers and Chicago Cubs at Wrigley Field

NATIONAL AMERICAN

N A

EAGUE LEAGUE

WORLD SERIES

945 25¢

downtown, brought his pet goat to the game. In some versions of the legend, the goat, beloved by fans, was a regular fixture in the stands that year, and was even known to "cheer" (in a goat-like fashion, at least) when good plays were made.

But when Sianis brought the goat to the World Series, he was asked to take the goat out of the stadium, because some fans were complaining about the smell. In response, an enraged Sianis put a curse on the Cubs that prevented them not only from winning the game that day, but from winning the Series against the Tigers, and from winning the pennant ever again.

At least a portion of the story is true, though the details are now shrouded in mystery.

Andy Frain was the head usher at the time; in 1928 he and his staff had taken over security at the park and cleaned up the stadium's old reputation as a place where ushers could be bribed to get you better seats. By the 1940s, the blue-and-gold uniformed Andy Frain ushers were a fixture of every sporting event in Chicago, and Frain's "code of honor" for ushers was well admired. His various bon mots, such as "never trust a man with a mustache or a man who carries an umbrella," were frequently repeated.

Fans lining up to buy World Series tickets at Wrigley Field in 1945

Expecting rowdy crowds for the World Series, Frain had equipped his ushers with "handy talky" radio sets so that any trouble could be quickly communicated among the 525 ushers and attendants who were employed to handle the sold-

Billy Sianis and his pet billy goat were ejected from Wrigley Field during Game 4 of the 1945 World Series

out stadium crowd. At the end of the game against Detroit, Frain told the press that he had trouble with only one fan: Billy Sianis, owner of a tavern described as "near Chicago Stadium." Sianis had insisted on being accompanied by a billy goat that he took into the box seat section, where it was paraded around wearing a blanket on which Sianis had attached a sign reading "We Got Detroit's Goat." Frain and Sianis seem to have argued; all the *Tribune* sports section said the next day was that "Frain finally convinced Sianis (that) goats should be with the Navy football teams." Another paper said that the goat was denied admission and that Sianis tied the goat to a post in the parking lot and attended the game himself.

No mention of a curse was made at the time, but over the years, the story began to spread. The Billy Goat Tavern moved from its original space in the Loop to its current "underground" space beneath Michigan Avenue (which is now called "the original" Billy Goat Tavern mainly for marketing reasons), where it became a hangout for reporters, who would gather after a day at the offices in the nearby buildings that housed both the *Tribune* and the *Chicago Sun Times*.

One such reporter was Mike Royko, one of Chicago's greatest writers and a 1972 recipient of the Pulitzer Prize for commentary. Over the course of his career, he wrote more than 7000 columns, at various times working for all three major papers (including the now defunct *Chicago Daily News*), and frequently wrote about his adventures in the Billy Goat Tavern. Though the Billy Goat sat only steps from the

lush hotel bars of the Magnificent Mile, it was not a fancy place, but an honest, low-down underground tavern full of shaky barstools, cracked Naugahyde, and wobbly tables. In Royko's columns, he portrayed it as a home away from home for philosopher drunks and wisecracking reporters in an era when hard drinking was practically a part of a reporter's job.

By the 1970s, the place was run by Sam Sianis, the nephew of the original owner, and Sam was known to retell the story of the goat at the World Series and the curse his uncle had placed on the team. In some versions of the story, Billy Sianis had been denied entrance and immediately placed a curse on the team, stating that they would never win the World Series, or play in another one, as long as Wrigley Field remained hostile to goats. In one version, Sianis had gone straight to a telegraph office and sent a telegram to Philip K. Wrigley stating "You are going to lose this World Series and you are never going to win another World Series again. You are never going to win a World Series again because you insulted my goat."

Royko repeated the story again and again in his columns, though in one of his last columns before his death in 1997, he said that the curse was actually nonsense; just a good story and nothing more. The real curse, he said, was brought down on the Cubs from above because the owners were reluctant to hire black ballplayers for years after Jackie Robinson

Mike Royko (right) and Sam Sianis at Billy Goat Tavern, 1981; and Jackie Robinson

Billy Goat Tavern, the Chicago sports fans' landmark

broke the color barrier. If a goat was to blame, he said, that goat had been sitting at an executive's desk in a gabardine suit. "(Wrigley) was known for . . . running the worst franchise in baseball," he wrote. "And a big part of that can be blamed on racism." The Cubs wouldn't hire any black players until 1953, nearly seven seasons after the Dodgers had added Robinson to the team.

But by then, columns about the curse were prominently displayed around the tavern, and, in an odd twist of fate, the tavern had become something of a tourist attraction in Chicago. Royko's faithful readers who came to the tavern in the early 1970s looking for "local color" occasionally wrote to express their dismay that the denizens they found were just sleepy bums slumped over stools (though Royko insisted that if they stuck around beyond the early afternoon hours, those bums might wake up and dazzle them with a monologue). But traffic increased, and got a lot more genteel, after John Belushi and Dan Aykroyd began doing skits about the place on *Saturday Night Live*, in which they imitated Sianis' broken English shouts of "Cheez borger, cheezborger! No Pepsi, Coke! No fries, chips!"

Sam Sianis, owner of the Billy Goat Tavern, with his goat, prior to the start of the National League playoff game between the Padres and the Cubs on Oct. 2, 1984

The tourists from locales beyond Royko's original readership read the columns on the wall, and the story spread further and further, eventually becoming one of the legends familiar not just to every Chicagoan, but to every baseball fan. When a series of unfortunate events narrowly cost the Cubs the pennant during the 2003 playoffs, media outlets throughout the country reported that the curse was alive and well. The fact that the Red Sox and White Sox shook off long losing streaks to win the Series in 2004 and 2005 only increased speculation that the Cubs' bad luck could only be the result of supernatural interference.

Over the years, many attempts have been made to undo the curse. Sam Sianis was brought to Wrigley Field—with a live goat—on opening day in both 1984 and 1989 (the Cubs won the division, but not the playoffs, both years), and on several other occasions, but it seemed like too little, too late. In 2003, a story circulated that a goat had been denied entrance to the stadium on the day that fan interference with a foul ball may have cost the team the pennant; the ball in question was purchased by Harry Caray's legendary Chicago Italian steakhouse, where chefs reduced it to ashes and mixed it into spaghetti sauce.

Fans continue to try all sorts of tricks to break the curse, but the Cubs continue to finish season after season looking, in Steve Goodman's words, like "the doormat of the National League." But fans still forgive them year after year, and pack the stadium every opening day hoping that *this* will be the year that the curse is finally broken. Wrigley Field, one of the last great stadiums from the golden age of baseball, is a national treasure, with its wonderful old-fashioned hand-operated scoreboard, a view from the upper deck that can't be beat, and the best "frosty malts" money can buy. Besides the baseball games, recent summer concerts at the stadium have been put on by Bruce Springsteen, Paul McCartney, and Pearl Jam.

WRIGLEY FIELD AND JACKIE ROBINSON

Today, Wrigley Field is the only still-active stadium where Jackie Robinson played. Royko attended the first game where Robinson appeared in Chicago and, according to one of his columns, caught a foul ball hit from Robinson's bat, which he sold to a man next to him in the stands for $10. Robinson won Rookie of the Year that year and led the Brooklyn Dodgers to the pennant.

CHAPTER 19.

THE LADY IN BLACK AT THE DRAKE HOTEL: MURDER AMID THE GLAMOUR BESIDE THE LAKE

1944

"Stop that crazy woman! She just shot my mother!"

The young woman screamed as a middle-aged woman in a black Persian lamb coat ran down the hall, clutching an antique pistol. In a posh suite in the hall, Adele Born Williams, society matron, lay dying of a gunshot wound to the head. And so began a mystery that would become one of the wildest stories of 1944, and one of Chicago's greatest unsolved crimes—in a city where that's really saying something.

Adele Born Williams had just returned to her luxurious apartment suite on the eighth floor of the Drake Hotel, the jewel in the crown of the Gold Coast, and still one of the most iconic hotels in the city. Upon entering her suite with her daughter, the mysterious woman in black emerged from the bathroom and started firing shots—apparently first at Mrs. Williams' daughter, but then at Mrs. Williams herself. The woman was no great shot; even at close range, only one of the bullets found their mark.

 Chicago Daily Tribune article on Jan 19, 1954 and vintage postcard of Drake Hotel (front right)

Voman Killer Keeps Guilty Secret

atron Slain in)rake Hotel 10 Years Ago

ɔw long can a woman keep ret? How long can a wom- ırdened by guilt resist the ing pangs of conscience? e are questions Chicago e ponder when they re- the mysterious murder of Adele Born Williams.

omewhere, probably in go," said John T. O'Mal- hief of detectives, "there oman—we called her the n in black—who remem- hat on this night 10 years he shot Mrs. Williams in rake hotel.

Clews Exhausted

hope her memory is vivid ıer conscience is strong. ong strain of silence and we hope, is working in avor. Maybe she will do hing to disclose her iden- We need some such break lve the crime. All the we had are exhausted. ng new has come to light ɔng time, tho our investi- ı has not been closed."

: murder of the wealthy, ly prominent matron of

Mrs. Adele Born Williams, whose slaying by woman in Drake hotel has remained unsolved for 10 years.

stairway with Mrs. Williams' daughter in close pursuit.

Daughter with Her

Mrs. Williams was the wife of Frank Starr Williams, a career attache of the state department. She and her daughter, Mrs. Patricia Goodbody, had been away from the hotel in the afternoon. They returned to their eighth floor room about 6:30 p. m.

Mrs. Patricia Goodbody, daughter of Mrs. Williams, who escaped uninjured as mother's slayer fired two shots at her.

and missed. Then she stepped into the suite and started firing wildly at Mrs. Williams. Mrs. Williams ran to grapple with her. The woman fired one more shot which struck Mrs. Williams in the head.

Runs from Room

The woman turned and ran down the corridor with Mrs. Goodbody running after her and shouting, "Stop that crazy woman, she shot my mother."

Two men, guests in the hotel,

(TRIBUNE Photos)

Pistol used in the shooting.

weapon—an old revolver manufactured before 1905.

Police had searched the stairway carefully right after the shooting. Apparently, police agreed, the woman or an accomplice had returned and discarded the gun while the building was crawling with policemen!

Find Missing Key

Equally baffling was the matter of the spare key to the suite. The assailant had entered the room with a key and immediately after the shooting police found the spare key missing from the desk key rack. Four hours later the key was found. No one saw it returned.

Mrs. Williams' daughter chased the woman down the hall, shouting for help. Two men saw her, and one of them could have stopped her, but he didn't. "I could have tripped her," he told the police. "But I'm not in the habit of tripping strange women."

Adele Born Williams survived just long enough to tell the police the story of what had happened, which was just as much a mystery to her as it was to anyone else. She hadn't recognized the "woman in black," and none of her jewelry was missing.

The police arrived on the scene at once, and promptly made a bungle of things, allowing all sorts of people who were simply curious to wander around the scene. They failed to apprehend any strange woman in black, and found no clues early on except for the fact that the key to Mrs. Williams' room was missing at the front desk.

Detective Quinn of the Chicago police immediately assumed that the whole thing was a hoax. "There was no woman in black," he sneered at Mrs. Williams' daughter. "*You* killed your mother, didn't you?" He had worked out a theory that Mrs. Williams had threatened to write her daughter out of her will, and, even though she was cutting her off, still loved her enough not to pinpoint her as her murderer. After the shot was fired, he believed, the two had quickly come up with a story about a woman in black. He seemed not to mind the fact that at least two witnesses had actually *seen* the woman in black.

The next day, things took a strange turn—the antique pistol was found at the bottom of a stairwell, in a space that the police had presumably searched the day before and found nothing. The key to the room mysteriously reappeared at the desk. A strange phone call was found to have been made, presumably by the shooter, from Mrs. Williams's suite to a nearby fish-and-ale house 20 minutes before the incident.

The story that the daughter had been the real killer was soon abandoned, and Mrs. Williams passed away in a hospital room the next day, making the case officially a homicide, not attempted murder.

From here, the case began to take several even stranger turns. The serial number on the gun connected it to a hold-up man who claimed to be the gun's original owner, but said that he had turned it in to the police years before. The police were never sure whether they believed that the gun was ever his—he had told them, by way of proof, that he had used it to shoot up the ground in a field near a railroad depot downstate years before, and the cops dutifully dug up the grounds he spoke of and found several bullets, but none were the right caliber to be fired from the gun.

The man himself was certainly not the killer, in any case: he had been in prison at the time of the crime. However, he did mention that some of his guns had been stolen by his sisters over the years.

And one of his sisters, a woman who called herself Ellen Murphy, was working as a key clerk at the Drake Hotel.

In fact, the man had *two* sisters at the Drake. One, Anna, was listed in the papers as a "hotel prowler," the kind of woman who hung around the hotel looking to drink with wealthy men. She had been cleared of murder raps before, but had a solid criminal record.

It was Ellen the key clerk, though, on whom most of the attention would center in coming days. She was living in the hotel with her lover, Patrick Murphy, the brother of the state labor director, whose last name she was using, though they were not married. Papers would call her Ellen Bennett, but her official name by then was Ellen Valanis-Bennett-Larksworthy-Welch.

At 41, to say that she'd lived an exciting life would be to put it very mildly. She had dropped out of school in sixth grade, married a man nearly four times her age when she was fifteen, then left him after six months, enrolling in college using a friend's diploma and giving birth to a son a few months later. Since then, she had been married a couple more times, always for very short periods, and to husbands who had a tendency to disappear. One husband was a man she met at a race track and who later had no memory of the whirlwind wedding. "When I woke up," he said, "I was in Dubuque, and I was married."

At least one of the husbands was murdered. Ellen was brought in for questioning, but was never formally a suspect in the still-unsolved crime. Her record was hardly clean, though; in 1939, she had borrowed one of her brother's guns, stolen a car that belonged to a state senator, put on a blonde wig, and attempted to hold a woman up in suburban Park Ridge—the car was found to be full of tapes and cords that she had planned to use to tie people up. When she was caught in the act, she claimed not to be Ellen Bennett at all, but a nightclub entertainer named Peggy Ryan.

In the early 1940s, she reconnected with her sister, who had spent some time as a call girl, and married another man who lived for only a few days after, and in 1942 she found a job working as the key clerk at the Drake (officials from which later admitted that they had neglected to do any sort of background check on the woman they knew as Mrs. Murphy). Even her friends said that she was a cold-blooded, calculated criminal who would go to great and dangerous lengths to grow her collection of diamonds and jewels.

Most everyone connected to the case began to theorize that Ellen had been in the room to steal the jewels and shot Mrs. Williams in a panic when she came back into the room. Ellen and her sister were both arrested twice in connection with the murder, and though Ellen admitted to owning a black Persian lamb coat, just like the one the killer wore, she swore she had never been in Mrs. Williams's room, and that she had been shopping in the Loop at the time the killing occurred.

Bennett and her sister both passed lie detector tests, and no charges against them ever seemed to stick—all evidence against them was strictly circumstantial. By the end of 1944, police had all but given up on the case, only holding out hope that somewhere, an old woman who owned a black fur coat had a terrible secret gnawing away at her conscience, and that one day she would come forward and confess.

That never happened. Though the papers re-ran the story every year on its anniversary for years, the unsolved case passed into history and was seldom mentioned in print after 1960—it survives today mainly as a ghost story. Some say that a ghostly woman in black has been seen haunting the eighth floor of the Drake Hotel; perhaps the ghost is a companion to the hotel's *other* resident ghost, the "woman in red" who is said to have haunted the tenth floor since committing suicide during a New Year's Eve party in 1920.

Vintage postcard of Coq d'Or

There is no evidence that the suicide in 1920 ever happened, and the "woman in black" ghost would be a particularly odd one, since the woman in black was the killer, not the victim. But why apply logic to the illogical? The mystery of the woman in black is just another of the countless secrets held by the venerable old Chicago hotels that line the lakeshore. Today, one can order an Old Fashioned at the Coq d'Or, the stately hotel bar where Ellen Bennett and her sister prowled decades ago.

The Drake Hotel is now free of murderers and "prowlers," and is, in fact, one of the classiest old-style hotels in town, and offers guests a true "big city" experience. The neon sign for the hotel that crowns the view of the city as you drive down Lake Shore Drive from the north side is as iconic a part of Chicago as anything else in the magnificent skyline.

CHAPTER 20.

BUGHOUSE SQUARE: WHERE PEOPLE TRIED TO CHANGE THE WORLD FROM ATOP A SOAPBOX

1947

Bernard Gavzer of Pennsylvania, a reporter for *The Bradford Era*, was stuck in Chicago in July of 1947, and surely must have wished he were anywhere else. Chicago in July wasn't much more pleasant than Chicago in January; the wind and snow were gone, but the close heat made a walk down the street feel like a swim in the river, and even on the near north side, the stench from the stockyards, fifty blocks to the south, was strong.

The news story of the year—maybe the century—was developing a thousand miles away. In Roswell, New Mexico, a flying saucer had crash-landed.

Flying saucers had been in the news for years by then; there was even a widely reported story of an "airship" being seen in Chicago 50 years earlier. But sightings had really picked up since World War II ended. Some speculated that ever since the atom bomb was dropped on Hiroshima, aliens from outer space wanted to know what these humans on the "Blue Planet" were up to.

 People listening to a speaker in north Chicago, 1942

The Deseret News

Salt Lake City, Utah, Wednesday Evening, July 9, 1947

Here's the Flying Saucer to End All Flying Saucers, *The Desert News*, July 9, 1947

Of course, most people didn't take the flying saucer stories all that seriously. But then came the crash in Roswell. This was no story of a pilot seeing "something strange," no hillbilly reporting strange lights in the sky over Georgia. An actual craft had crash-landed, and witnesses even said that they had seen the aliens lying dead on the ground.

Reporters stuck in Chicago couldn't add much to the story from so far away. There wasn't much to cover in Chicago at all, in fact. Other than the flying saucer, it was a pretty slow week for news. Having not much to do with his copious spare time other than sit in the dingy near north bars, drinking the night away, the poor reporter from the *Bradford Era* must have cursed his luck at being so far from Roswell.

Late that evening, Gavzer wandered into Bughouse Square, the little park on Clark Street, just above Chicago Avenue, and found himself in the midst of a circus.

There was a man swallowing fire, another walked around with a chicken on his head. Peanut and hot dog vendors wheeled carts around. And everywhere, there were soapboxes, topped by wild-eyed cranks, all shouting at the top of their lungs about—what else?—the flying saucers.

Had Gavzer asked someone in the back of the large crowd what was going on, he would have been told that he had arrived in Bughouse Square, "Chicago's refuge for self-styled intellectuals." Officially known as Washington Square, this small square just north of the Loop was the oldest known park in the city, and tradition held that anyone who wanted to was allowed to make a speech there at any time. Any night when the weather was good, soapbox orators would hold court for a crowd of rowdy hecklers. Some said it was the best entertainment in the city; years later, legendary columnist Mike Royko would say that it was the perfect place for tourists: for no money at all, they could spend half an hour in the park, then go home to their quiet towns and say they had seen a dirty man make a speech about free love right out in public.

Gavzer couldn't dig up any new information on the flying saucer itself, but he could report what the biggest cranks in town were saying about it.

When Gavzer first arrived, a one-armed man was standing up to make his speech. He was known as "One Armed Charlie, king of the soapboxers." He had the constitution memorized, and was known to answer questions about it while standing on his head. He was an expert at dealing with hecklers, for whom his favorite retort was "if brains were bug juice, you couldn't drown a gnat!" But tonight, he was talking about UFO sightings.

Washington (Bughouse) Square Park

A woman speaking to the crowd from atop her soapbox, c. 1912

"This is nothing more than mass hysteria," Charlie railed, waving his right arm. "And the terrible thing about mass hysteria is that the more water you throw on it, the more it burns!"

The flying saucers, he stated, were just "visions." "These visions," he stated, "can be erased by healthy living. But to be healthy, you've got to eat living things. I eat 50 dandelion buds a day when they're in season!"

On the next soapbox over stood a dashing fellow known as The Cosmic Kid, a soapbox philosopher who was said to take his audience on "flights of fancy to empyrean realms of thought," and made a good living by passing his hat around after the speeches. Upon his death a few years later, The Chicago Druid Society would give him a Druid-style funeral in the park. On the night of the Roswell debate, The Cosmic Kid stated that the flying discs were evidence of life on other planets.

"Science has a wide open view of the possibility that life exists on other planets," said the Cosmic Kid. The crowd clapped and shouted, but the kid was just getting warmed up. "The people of Mars," he said, "have an understanding of the cosmic process in advance of ours, and have a theory that the interpenetration of radiation of energy into interstellar space holds the solar systems together. The Martians are now making explorations to prove their cosmic theory, and this explains the flying saucers."

"All that in one breath!" Gavner wrote.

Across the park, a skinny, scantily clad old woman was raising her arms, screaming Jesus's name—nearly every writer who ever went to Bughouse Square wrote about this woman, who was variously called "Weird Mary" and "Crazy Mary." Most of the people ignored her, like an act they had seen a thousand times, and focused on the Martians.

The Cosmic Kid yielded his soapbox to a scruffy hobo named Porkchops Charlie, a "knight of the open road."

"I've seen flying discs plenty of times!" he shouted.

"When you were drunk? Me too!" shouted a heckler.

"Mostly when I'm in the boxcars," Porkchops said, matter-of-factly. "I believe that the saucers are moving shadows between the sun and earth that deceive the eye because of their electric vibration."

"Ohh, Jesus!" shouted the old woman. "He's a-coming! Judgment day is upon us!"

"Yeah? asked a heckler. "Is he coming in a flying saucer, or just floating down on his own?"

"He's a-coming! You've got to repent!" she screamed.

"You've got it all wrong," another guy shouted to Porkchops. "Those saucers are just plates carrying T-Bone steaks. Maybe it's those ENIACS—you know, those thinking machines invested at Harvard and Princeton—that are doing some thinking and inventing on their own!"

"That doesn't make the tiniest bit of sense!" shouted One-Armed Charlie.

"If the machines can almost think," the man explained, "it's reasonable to believe they could think of something like flying saucers that not even our scientists can match."

Gavzer scribbled until his notepad was full. He wired his story back to

Newberry Library

Bradford just as they were setting the type for the lead story of the next day—that the flying saucers were, in fact, nothing more than weather balloons.

This seems to have been a pretty typical evening in Bughouse Square, if a relatively tame one; now and then a riot would break out. For the better part of a century, the park remained a refuge for hobos and "self-styled" intellectuals. Some real old timers say that radio killed Bughouse Square, but people in Chicago today still maintain that it was still active well into the radio era, such as the night in the 1940s when the *Bradford Era's* reporter was there. Most maintain that it was actually television that killed the square—the practice of speaking there was never outlawed or formally ended; it simply died around 1960. In 1972, one of the regulars revisited the scene and was asked by reporters if he thought the park could rise again. "Doesn't have to," he said with a chuckle. "The whole world is Bughouse Square now."

The park sits on Clark Street, just a couple of blocks north of Chicago Avenue, in the shadow of the Magnificent Mile. Today it is mostly a park for old men in overcoats and young Gold Coast couples walking dogs, but every summer, typically the last Saturday in July, the adjacent Newberry Library sponsors The Bughouse Square Debates, at which the soapboxes are brought back. The event attracts several old regulars from the park's glory days, and, true to form, it seems to attract every weirdo and conspiracy theorist in town. In 1988, the *Chicago Sun Times* called it "a megadose of top-drawer rhetorical wrestlemania."

FREE SPEECH PARK

Bughouse Square was one of around 20 or 30 "free speech parks" and "open forums" that operated around the city around the 1920s; its south side equivalent was the Bug Club in Washington Park.

Two Bughouse Square regulars, William Lloyd Smith and Joffre Stuart, were the nominees for president and vice president for the Beatnik Party in 1960. Smith, an anarchist, promised to dissolve the government and resign upon his election. Stuart was still appearing at annual Bughouse Square debates nearly 50 years later, passing out leaflets about conspiracy theories

CHAPTER 21.

CHESS RECORDS AND THE CHICAGO BLUES: THERE WAS NO OTHER SOUND LIKE THE CHESS RECORDS SOUND

1950-75

In 1972, executives at Chess Records in Chicago must have been scratching their heads. The founders, Leonard and Phil Chess, had both died, and the company was just on the verge of being consigned to history as another old blues label. But all of a sudden, as they were breathing their last, their latest release had gone to the top of the charts. For the first time ever, a Chess Records release was the No. 1 record in the country.

Chess Records had become a legend for releasing game-changing jazz and blues records. Some of the most seminal artists on the planet had released some of their most vital music on Chess. But now, the artist who was bringing them to No. 1 was Chuck Berry. He had been a groundbreaking pioneer once upon a time, back in the 1950s, and his song "Maybelline" had been Chess's first hit. But for years Berry had been regarded as a has-been with nothing new to say. And the song in question wasn't exactly the sort of track that would make people re-evaluate Berry's status: it was "My Ding a Ling," a novelty song full of cheap double (well, single) entendres and corny jokes. It was so bad

 The Best of Muddy Waters, 1958; Moanin' in the Moonlight, Howlin' Wolf, 1959; Bo Diddley, 1958; Best of Little Walter, 1958; At Last, Etta James, 1960; The London Chuck Berry Sessions, 1972

best of MUDDY WATERS
LP 1427
howlin' wolf
moanin' in the moonlight
BO DIDDLEY
THE BEST OF
LITTLE WALTER
ETTA JAMES
at last!
THE LONDON CHUCK BERRY SESSION

Leonard, Marshall, Phil Chess, and the Chess Recording Studio

that one disc jockey is said to have introduced it by saying "Oh, Chuck Berry, how could you?"

And yet, this was the first No. 1 record released by Chess Records. In the end, it proved to be their last release.

In a way, they ended on a winning note. In another, though, it was a sad, strange end to a label that helped forever cement Chicago in the public imagination as the home of the blues.

The founders, a pair of Polish-born Jewish brothers named Leonard and Phil Chess, came to Chicago in 1928 and opened a string of liquor stores and night clubs on the south side, the biggest of which often featured live entertainment by jazz and blues artists. Ella Fitzgerald entertained at the store early in her career. The brothers loved the music, and in the late 1940s they started a record label of their own, taking the name Chess Records in 1950.

Though their background was in liquor sales, the brothers shared a fine ear for music and an instinct for what would sell, and the company was run by the two of them with little help from anyone. They set up their own recording studio, scouted talent, produced recordings, packaged the records in the sleeves, and even sold them by hand. On at least one occasion, Leonard even played bass drum on a session when no bass drummer could be found. They made frequent trips to sell records and scout new talent in the southeast U.S., where blues music was more established, but they opened their studio in a narrow two-story building at 2120 South Michigan Avenue.

In between trips, they would scour local Chicago bars with tape recorders, always on the lookout for new talent. Their first major find was Muddy Waters, who was, at the time, playing gigs at night and driving a truck during the day. "Chicago had a big black population from World War II," remembered Marshall Chess, Leonard's son, who began working for the label at 10. "In the south, there were these clubs called juke joints where they played the acoustic blues, and they came up to Chicago to make a better life, to make money, like my family came from Poland."

Marshall had a front row seat to watch the fledgling label attract a whole stable of revolutionary talent. Before long, Chess Records had signed jazz, blues, and early rock 'n' roll icons such as Howlin' Wolf, Chuck Berry, Bo Diddley, Etta James, Little Walter, and Willie Dixon. Though not exactly a rock label, the influence of Chess Records on the birth of rock 'n' roll music cannot be overstated. "The thing about Chess that's so amazing," Marshall recalled "is that we had Beethoven, Bach and Mozart on the same label." Though they lacked training in production and sound engineering, the two brothers created the famous "Chess Records sound," which was characterized by a booming echo that they created by connecting microphones to speakers with a sewer pipe.

Soon, with the growing electric blues scene on which Chess was at the forefront, Chess Records became the dominant independent record label in Chicago.

Marshall remembered vividly the time they first realized that their artists were crossing over into mainstream success—i.e., success outside of strictly black markets. "We noticed it in 1955—we were riding along in the car and all of a sudden we heard Chuck Berry's first record, "Maybellene," on WIND, the pure white station, and my Dad just lit up."

In 1964, The Rolling Stones, who had taken their name from a Muddy Waters song, were still just an upstart band from London with a couple

of hits under their belt. They idolized Chess Records and the Chess Records sound, and their manager, Andrew Oldham, asked if his young band could use the hallowed Chess studio for a few sessions for their own label.

Only Chess Records artists were allowed to use the Chess Records facilities, but when Oldham got in touch with teenage Marshall, he found that the young man was receptive to breaking the rules for the Stones. A few sessions were arranged, and, according to legend, Muddy Waters himself, the man who gave The Rolling Stones their name, helped them haul their guitars and amplifiers up the staircase into the studio.

"It is certainly possible," Marshall later wrote, "that Muddy might have helped the Stones lug some equipment from the parking lot into the studios, because he was that kind of a guy. The blues musicians weren't too interested in The Rolling Stones, but they did like the fact that they were covering their songs, and that, as a result, more and more people, particularly white people, would become aware of their music." Willie Dixon supposedly came by the studio to try to sell the youngsters a few songs. At the end of May, 1964, only days after the session, Muddy Waters cheerfully told *Melody Maker* magazine that "They're my boys. I like their version of 'I Just Want To Make Love To You.' They fade it out just like we did."

The Rolling Stones: 2120 South Michigan Avenue, Recorded Live at Chess Studio, June 10 & 11, 1964.

The Stones recorded more than a dozen tracks, mainly blues standards, over three sessions at the studio, one of which, "It's All Over Now," went to No. 1 in the U.K. Mick Jagger was especially pleased with the sound.

"Andrew (our manager) didn't know anything about the blues," he later recalled. "The cat who really got it together was Ron Malo, the engineer for Chess. He had been on all the original sessions."

Chuck Berry in 1957

Drummer Charlie Watts said similar things in the summer of 1964. "The biggest advantage of recording strong rhythm and blues in Chicago," he said, "was that the engineers were a lot more used to that sort of music. I don't think anyone anywhere could record this type of music as effectively as they did in Chicago."

The Stones returned to Chess in November of 1964, and then again in May of 1965, where Ron Malo helped them work through the night recording "(I Can't Get No) Satisfaction," their biggest hit (the recording would be finished at RCA in Hollywood). It reached number one in both the U.S. and U.K., something no record on the Chess Label had ever done at the time.

By then the company was starting to run out of steam, and the brothers sold the company for $6.5 million in 1969, shortly before Leonard's death of an apparent heart attack at the age of 52. By 1972, when they finally scored a No. 1 hit with Chuck Berry's "My Ding a Ling" (a live recording from which the iconic Chess sound was absent), the company was on its last legs. "My Ding a Ling" is considered their "swan song" release.

Marshall Chess went on to work with The Rolling Stones extensively around the time that Chess went under; he is listed as executive producer on such albums as *Sticky Fingers* and *Exile on Main Street*. A decade after "My Ding a Ling," he began to lament that much of the

Chess catalog was no longer available at all, and began the long process of having the early recordings reissued. Several boxed sets now cover a huge range of the Chess Records recordings.

Since 2007, Marshall Chess has been hosting the "Chess Records Hour" on Sirius Satellite Radio. Chess Records now exists only as a memory and a landmark in Chicago—and music—history, but Marshall and his own son, Jamar Chess, continue to produce, record and promote music today.

The Chess Records building at 2120 South Michigan Avenue was designated a Chicago landmark in 1990. It is now the home of Willie Dixon's Blues Heaven, a foundation to encourage the next generation of blues musicians and singers by providing scholarships, grants, music clinics and festivals. The foundation also supports senior blues musicians. Members of Dixon's family conduct tours in the afternoon, Mondays through Saturdays.

Muddy Waters

CHAPTER 22.

MAYOR DALEY THE FIRST: 7,183 DAYS OF THE LAST OF THE BIG CITY BOSSES

1955-1976

Tension ran high in Chicago in 1968, as the Democratic National Convention approached. The year 1968 was a bad time for American cities to begin with, going down as a summer of riots and assassinations, and Mayor Daley of Chicago didn't quiet things down much by telling police officers to "shoot to kill any arsonist" during the riots that followed the assassination of Martin Luther King, Jr. Specifically, he told them to kill "any arsonist or anyone with a Molotov cocktail in his hand, because they're potential murderers," but they were only to "shoot to maim" looters. Giving the police such vague, yet harsh, instructions was a chilling move. He later backtracked and said "there wasn't any shoot-to-kill order. That was a fabrication," but he said this after a conference in which he stated that he had "very emphatically and very definitely" ordered just such a rule.

Such a turnaround, such a method of rearranging the facts to his own convenience, was characteristic of Mayor Richard J. Daley, who controlled Chicago for a generation. To some he was not so much a mayor as a pharaoh—a long-serving ruler whose word was absolute.

 Mayor Richard J. Daley at an election campaign rally, 1975

D FOR CHIC
Richard J. DAL
SWAYS &
RANSIT
OGRAMS
MAYOR
DALEY

Police attack protesters outside of the 1968 Democratic National Convention; and Mayor Richard J. Daley pumps his fist as he speaks from the floor.

Throughout his reign as mayor, which lasted from 1955 until his death in 1976, he was the unquestioned boss of the city, sometimes known ominously as "The Man on Five," because of his fifth-floor office. At meetings, aldermen would generally vote for his proposals nearly unanimously (with only Alderman Leon Depres, his long-suffering rival, defecting). His son would serve an even longer term as mayor, and the name "Daley" is still everywhere in Chicago, on buildings and institutions. Theirs is a dynasty that could only be rivaled by Carter Harrison and his son, in the late 1800s and early 1900s. But it is Mayor Daley the First who became known as The Pharaoh.

In the run-up to the 1968 Democratic National Convention, which was to be held at the International Amphitheatre in Chicago, there were many signs of grim unrest. With President Lyndon B. Johnson declining to run again, and with the primary season upended by the assassination of Senator Robert Kennedy, Chicago became ground zero for anti-war protestors, and rumors swirled that some of them were going to spike the city drinking water with LSD. An atmosphere of paranoia pervaded the scene, and anti-war protesters descended upon the city to protest the likely nomination of Hubert Humphrey, a pro-war candidate then running against the anti-war Eugene McCarthy (as well as a plethora of other candidates; the 1968 convention was perhaps the last in modern history in which the nomination was still wide open at the time of the convention).

As police presence was beefed up in the city around the protests, the protesters chanted "the whole world is watching" as the cameras showed police appearing to beat up anyone who looked vaguely like a radical. Even journalists were not safe—both Dan Rather and Mike Wallace were roughed up by the police. Many of the protesters were, indeed, out of control, but to many, it seemed that the police had simply been given *carte blanche* to attack whomever they pleased, and few argued that the police behaved any better than the protesters did. Daley's reputation wasn't helped by the fact that, as a speaker spoke during the Convention against the "Gestapo in the streets of Chicago," Daley was shown muttering what lip readers said was an anti-Semitic remark. When he tried to defend his actions regarding the police, he slipped into one of his trademark gaffes: "Gentlemen, let's get this thing straight, once and for all. The policeman is not here to create disorder. The policeman is here to *preserve* disorder." He meant "order," but some said that his actual statement was more appropriate.

However, though the whole world *was* watching, most of Middle America seemed to take Daley's side. His chosen candidate, Humphrey, was nominated to run against Richard Nixon (to whom he would ultimately lose), and Daley would go on to be re-elected in 1971 for another term. But the mayor's popularity had taken a hit. Some said that it was his own power and influence that had gotten John F. Kennedy elected in 1960, but his failure to truly get the city, and the Convention, under control in 1968 had handed the election to Nixon.

Daley is now sometimes called "The Last of the Big City Bosses," a tough-talking, plain speaking "man of the people" who "got things done." And these included things that a mayor more concerned with the actual political process might not have been able to accomplish. Under his watch, in an era when many other midwestern cities, such as Detroit and Cleveland, began to collapse, Chicago endured, keeping a double-A bond rating when other cities were falling into fiscal crises.

Born in 1902 in Bridgeport, the working-class Irish neighborhood on the south side, Daley was the son of a sheet metal worker and a former suffragette. He worked as a young man as a newspaper delivery boy and a door-to-door salesman, and even worked for a time in the Union

Stockyards. After obtaining a law degree he practiced law, but by then he was already involved in politics, the field that would occupy most of his life.

In 1936, young Daley served a term in the state House of Representatives. He served this term as a Republican, though this was just a matter of opportunism, as he was a lifelong Democrat (most Chicagoans will tell you that party affiliation among city government is sort of odd and arbitrary; in the most recent open mayoral election, there were conservatives and liberals running, but everyone was a Democrat). After serving in various local and state-level positions, including Cook County Clerk, Daley was narrowly elected mayor in 1955, and by the end of his first term was known as one of the most powerful mayors in the country.

Many objected to his methods, and Daley seemed to inspire love and hate in equal over-sized measures, but it is hard to argue with his achievements; under his tenure, Chicago built most of its most famous skyscrapers, including the Sears Tower (then the tallest building in the world), O'Hare International Airport, McCormick Place, the campus of the University of Illinois at Chicago, and countless infrastructure projects.

Chicago's politics were truly a "machine" during his tenure, and Daley kept it running smoothly, making sure that Chicago was "the city that works."

Mayor Richard J. Daley with his family November, 1955

His record was far from spotless, however, and he became a target for the left-wing of his own party after the riots of 1968. In 1972, nominee George McGovern kept Daley out of the Democratic

Convention altogether. In the following years, rumors and evidence swirled implicating the mayor in various charges of corruption in city government. None of this was enough to cost him re-election, but his reputation and legacy were badly damaged. Mike Royko, perhaps the city's most beloved columnist, wrote a particularly damning biography, *Boss*, that Daley himself tried to suppress. One story goes that when the book hit stores, the mayor ran around to book shops personally tearing copies of the book to bits.

Mayor Richard J. Daley views Chicago's 1966 skyline from atop the then new Daley Center

Despite all of these problems, it is likely that "the Man on Five" could have continued to be re-elected to the office as many times as he liked if his reign had not been halted by his death. In December, 1976, Daley suffered a heart attack in his doctor's office at 900 North Michigan Avenue, right on the "Magnificent Mile" that came into its own during his tenure, and he was pronounced dead at a nearby hospital 90 minutes later, putting an end to a remarkable term that had lasted 7,183 days. His fame was, by then, international; the *Tribune* wrote in his obituary that Chicagoans traveling abroad had been amazed to find out how much foreigners knew about Mayor Daley.

His place as mayor was taken by Michael A. Bilandic, who served the remainder of a term marked by labor strikes. He was followed by the term of Jane Byrne (1979), the first female mayor, and Harold Washington (1983), the first black mayor, whose own term was also interrupted by a fatal heart attack in 1987. In the next election that followed in 1989, Daley's son, Richard M. Daley, was elected, and he

Mayor Richard J. Daley and Queen Elizabeth II during her 1959 visit to Chicago

would serve until 2011, stepping down only shortly after breaking his father's record as longest-serving mayor after more than two decades on the job. One of Daley's other sons, William Daley, served as President Obama's chief of staff in 2011.

Daley may not have died with an unblemished record, but his policies of urban renewal may have saved the city from collapse in an era when many other cities did just that. Some believe that it was his strength as mayor that kept Chicago as a world-class city in the late 20th century.

NEIGHBORHOOD OF MAYORS

Bridgeport was long considered "the neighborhood of mayors," as no less than five 20th-century mayors came from the area. Go to Schaller's Pump at 3714 South Halsted Street, the oldest restaurant in the city (which was sometimes considered "the second office" for Bridgeport mayors—the 11th district Democratic office is right across the street) to see portraits of various mayors hanging on the wall. Jack Schaller, a third generation owner who lives above the bar, can still often be found hanging around the bar, and is usually happy to gossip about the former mayors. Try the butt steak sandwich, but be prepared to fight crowds if you come anywhere near a White Sox game. The stadium is down the road.

OLD CHICAGO SCENE: North Michigan Avenue, 1929

CHAPTER 23.

OPRAH AND EBERT AT THE MOVIES: TWO CHICAGO ICONS AND THE DATE THAT MADE HISTORY

1986

In the early 1980s, Oprah Winfrey and Roger Ebert went out on a date. After a movie (of course), they went to a modest dinner at a local Hamburger Hamlet.

“I don't know what to do, Roger,” said Oprah. “The ABC stations want to syndicate my show. So does King World.”

This was a dilemma, to be sure. If the show wasn't a success right away, ABC could at least keep her on the air. King World could bring her bigger numbers, but if she wasn't successful, she would be off the air in three months.

Oprah was, at the time, the new host of the local *AM Chicago*, where her show was getting better ratings than *Donahue*, its rival. Ebert himself had been an institution in Chicago since the late 1960s, when he began writing film reviews for the *Chicago Sun Times*, a job that would earn him a Pulitzer Prize. He had become nationally famous with his own syndicated show, *At the Movies*, in which he and Gene Siskel, the other major film critic in

---

 Oprah Winfrey with Will Smith, at the time known for his role in *The Fresh Prince Of Bel-Air; A Night At The Oprah*, 1992

Gene Siskel and Roger Ebert, 1982

Chicago, would show previews of new movies and argue about whether or not they were any good.

There had never been a show quite like Siskel and Ebert's. Like a lot of great Chicago television personalities, they didn't *look* as though they belonged on television. They looked like the kind of guys who would sit next to you on the El, or at Hamburger Hamlet. But there's always been a peculiar thing with Chicago television personalities—Chicago is a city that tends to put people on the air not because they're "camera ready," but because they know what they're talking about. Siskel and Ebert knew movies, and their enthusiasm (or lack thereof, if a movie was bad) was infectious.

Ebert had met Oprah when he and Siskel appeared on a show she had hosted in Baltimore, along with a chef who sprayed blended zucchini all over the place and four little people in chipmunk costumes who danced with hula-hoops while singing "The Chipmunk Christmas Song." Ebert had been impressed with Oprah's grace and skill with handling such an odd assortment of guests, and felt that she was a natural who belonged on television.

So, that night in Hamburger Hamlet, Ebert took out a pen and a napkin, and gave her some advice that would change television history.

On line one, he wrote down how much he made in a year doing his show in syndication.

On line two he doubled it, reasoning that she would get twice as much since she wouldn't have to split the pay with Siskel, like he did.

On line three he doubled *that,* because her show would be an hour long, not half an hour, like his.

On line four, he multiplied *that* figure by five, because she would be on five days a week instead of one.

And on line five, he doubled *that* figure, because he assumed that Oprah's ratings would probably be twice as big as the ratings that he and Gene pulled in doing *Siskel and Ebert.*

Oprah looked at the napkin for a few seconds, then told Roger she was going with King World.

Looking back on the date more than 20 years later, Ebert noted that he probably should have added another "times 20." His instincts had told him that her show would be a success, but no one could have predicted Oprah's meteoric rise; she became one of Chicago's greatest success stories. Her name would arguably become as connected to the image people had of Chicago as Al Capone—and her influence was a lot more positive than Capone's.

Roger Ebert and Oprah Winfrey

Born in 1954 to an impoverished family in rural Mississippi, Oprah came from hardscrabble roots. She survived sexual abuse and pregnancy at the age of 14, and then migrated from her mother's family to her father's in Tennessee. In high school she found a job in radio and was such a natural in broadcasting that she found herself co-anchoring the local news before she was even 20 years old. Her popularity and abilities there got her a job hosting a morning talk show program, and her success caught the eye of the producers of *AM Chicago*, which she joined in 1983. Soon, she took the program from third place to first in its time slot.

Taking the advice of Ebert to go into syndication, she launched the hour-long *The Oprah Winfrey* show in 1986. Though early reviewers and ratings-watchers saw her in a terrific battle for ratings with the then top-rated *Phil Donahue* show, she was soon pulling in twice Donahue's ratings and revolutionized the talk show format, which had previously been a format dominated by white male hosts. Her show aired for 25 years, airing its last episode in 2011 when Oprah decided to move on to focus on her own television channel.

Ebert's prediction that she would be twice as popular as *Siskel and Ebert* proved to be a little off the mark—his later estimate that he should have added "times twenty" may have actually been shy of Oprah's actual popularity. Today, she is one of the richest women in the world, and for a time was the world's only black billionaire. Many consider her the most influential woman in the world; it was estimated that her support for Barack Obama in the hotly contested 2008 primary campaign got him a million votes, clinching him the nomination over Hillary Clinton.

This is not to say that Gene Siskel and Roger Ebert did badly. Roger and Oprah only went out on a couple of dates, though they remained friends and co-hosted the Chicago Emmy Awards in 1986. Ebert would continue his successful show for another two decades, employing a variety of guest hosts after Siskel's death of brain cancer in 1999 before eventually hiring Richard Roeper, a fellow *Sun Times* columnist, as a permanent co-host. Though health issues cost Ebert his ability to speak, he continued to write film reviews, and his blog and Twitter feed were among the most successful on the Internet at the time of his death in 2013. In 2011, his autobiography was an instant best seller.

Today, the Gene Siskel Film Center is on North State Street, just above Randolph, catering mostly to film buffs and film students with its screenings of new and classic films. Not to be outdone, a plaque honoring Roger Ebert sits on the sidewalk across the street below the marquee of the famous

Harpo Studios

Chicago Theatre.

Tour guides note that one of the first questions they get is still "Where does Oprah live?" It is a difficult question to answer, since she has property all over the city (and the rest of the country). Some say she has the penthouse at Lake View Tower, the single condo building that sits east of Lake Shore Drive near Navy Pier. Others say she has the top two floors of Water Tower Place on Michigan Avenue.

The building that will forever be associated with her, though, is Harpo Studios, where her famous show was filmed until 2011. It sits a mile or so west of the Loop at Randolph and Aberdeen, and is still sometimes used for production of other shows, though its post-Oprah future has not yet been determined.

Perhaps the most obvious change for longtime residents was what Harpo Studios did to the west Loop area. Madison Street, only a block away from the building into which Oprah moved to establish her studio, had been known as "skid row" for decades, a slum inhabited almost entirely by alcoholic men. Nearly every building in the vicinity was either a saloon or a flophouse. Even today one can still sometimes see the occasional faded sign painted on a wall advertising transient hotels with adult movies available in the rooms—and those were just the classier places. The less classy ones offered single rooms divided by chicken wire. The area was already slowly turning around when Oprah moved in, but today "skid row" is unrecognizable. Randolph, Washington and Madison are lined with trendy restaurants, luxury lofts, art galleries and boutiques. It is hard to imagine a single flophouse operating in the vicinity.

OPRAH, EBERT AND MOVIES

Oprah Winfrey in *The Color Purple*, 1985

Oprah has occasionally acted in movies herself, including a starring role in *The Color Purple*, and voice work in animated movies such as *The Princess and the Frog*, *Charlotte's Web*, and *Bee Movie*.

Oprah recalled, "So, I got the book section and I read this review of Alice Walker's book, *The Color Purple*. I was in my pajamas, and I put my coat on, over my pajamas, and went to the book store. I got the book and read it, in one day."

Ebert occasionally worked as a screenwriter early in his career; his most famous work is the screenplay for *Beyond the Valley of the Dolls*. He was hired at one point to write a script for *Who Killed Bambi*, which was to be a starring vehicle for the band The Sex Pistols. It was never released, but Ebert posted the script on his blog in 2010.

OLD CHICAGO SCENE: Union Station concourse, 1943

CHAPTER 24.

BARACK OBAMA, CHICAGO PRESIDENT: HIS ELECTION NIGHT RALLY IN GRANT PARK MADE HISTORY

2008

In November, 2008, a crowd of more than 200,000 people gathered in Grant Park on election night. It was unseasonably warm that night; and the mood was electric. All the polls pointed to Chicago's own junior Senator, Barack Obama, winning the presidency. Some noted that the simple fact that they were outdoors at night in November without being cold was an indication that something miraculous was happening.

Only five years before, few had ever heard of Barack Obama, a state senator and lawyer who taught constitutional law at the University of Chicago. Rumor had it that the Democratic Party had plans to make him the next mayor of Chicago if Richard M. Daley ever stepped down from the post.

However, after a failed bid for a seat in the House of Representatives in 2000, Obama began to assess his chances at winning a seat in the Senate, and announced his campaign in 2003, thrilling crowds with speeches in which he denounced the war in Iraq, which was just getting under way, and still held broad popular support around the country

 Barack Obama at his U.S. Presidential Election Victory Speech and Celebration at Grant Park, November 4, 2008

Obama's victory address surrounded by a huge crowd of 200,000 people in Chicago's Grant Park

at the time. When the public attitude toward the war began to sour, Obama was one of the few politicians who could claim to have been against it from the start.

When Jack Ryan, his expected Republican opponent, pulled out of the race in June, 2004, following an alleged sex scandal, it seemed as if Obama was running unopposed. Alan Keyes, a politician and radio talk show host, was brought in as the new Republican nominee, but most knew that Keyes, whose fiercely right-wing views had never brought him broad cross-over appeal, never had a chance.

Obama was still relatively unknown outside of Chicago when he was offered a chance to speak at the Democratic National Convention, but his soaring keynote speech was seen by more than nine million viewers. In the speech, he told his own story—born in Hawaii to a Kenyan goat herder father and a Kansas-born mother, who gave him the African name of Barack, meaning "blessed," confident in her belief that in America, a strange name would not be a barrier to success.

His parents, who were not wealthy, could hardly have dreamed of just how successful their son would be. He won a scholarship to Harvard, came to Chicago as a community organizer, and was now coasting to victory in a Senate election, and telling a packed stadium and millions of viewers that "There's not a black America and white America and Latino America and Asian America; there's the United States of America."

On *The Daily Show* the next day, Jon Stewart showed clips of various speakers from the Convention touting their humble backgrounds.

Speaker after speaker proudly claimed to be the son of a mill worker, a factory worker, or a teacher. Then he showed the clip of Obama saying that his father was a Kenyan goat herder. "He wins!" said Stewart.

Before the birth of the United States, the sheer notion that a goat herder's son could become the leader of the free world would have seemed absurd. But Obama's Convention speech was a huge success, and within days, Roger Ebert appeared on a radio show speaking effusively about the young senatorial candidate who he believed would be the first black president of the United States. His sentiments were echoed elsewhere.

After John Kerry, the candidate Obama was supporting with this speech, went on to lose the general election of 2004, the Democratic nomination for 2008 was seen as wide open. Everyone knew Hillary Clinton was planning to run, but some Democratic activists, perhaps suffering from "Clinton-Bush Fatigue," hoped for a fresher face, one the Republicans had not been preparing to fight for years.

Obama was initially resistant to the idea of running for president so soon after his landslide election to the senate, but when he traveled the country on a tour to promote his new book, *The Audacity of Hope*, people begged him to run for president wherever he went. In February, 2007, he announced his candidacy.

He was still considered a long-shot candidate, though, and many believed that he was simply hoping to get the vice presidential nomination. But he and Clinton gradually emerged as the dominant candidates, and in a stunning upset, he won the Iowa Caucus, the first major event of the primary season. For several months, the primary battle dragged on, as Obama and Clinton fought bitterly for delegates. But in the end, Obama won the day, and in 2008 he was named the Democratic Party's nominee for the presidency.

As Obama went on to run a nearly flawless campaign, his Republican opponent John McCain suffered a series of missteps, stemming partly from his own inability to excite audiences the way Obama did, and partly from his being unable to shake off the ghost of then-president

George W. Bush, who had become increasingly unpopular throughout his second term. When the economy crashed in the fall of 2008, McCain's gambit of suspending his campaign to focus on the crisis did not work as well as he had hoped, and voters saw him as erratic. His initial strength as a candidate had been his vast experience in politics compared to the freshman senator, but this argument was undermined when he chose Sarah Palin, the first-term governor of Alaska, as his running mate. Obama had had the entire primary season to find his footing as a candidate and national figure; Palin's lack of practice in a national campaign was evident. Though some thought that adding Palin to the ticket would be the "game changer" that McCain needed, the gamble didn't pay off in the end, and Palin became a polarizing figure after a promising start.

By election night, the polls were all very clear—Obama was poised to win the election by a large margin. On that night, McCain organized a small rally whose mood appeared somber, and the Obama campaign reserved the whole of Chicago's Grant Park.

The park is an area rich with history. If they looked behind them onto Michigan Avenue, attendees could see the Chicago Auditorium, where Theodore Roosevelt first gave his "speak softly and carry a big stick" speech. They could see the Orchestra Hall at Symphony Center where Dr. Martin Luther King, Jr., spoke several times (including a speech attended by a young Hillary Clinton). Michigan Avenue itself was the route of Abraham Lincoln's funeral carriage. The park was the site of riots during the tumultuous Democratic National Convention of 1968, where police attacked protesters as onlookers chanted "The whole world is watching."

Now, 40 years later, the whole world was watching again.

The crowd in the park on election night was estimated to be around 240,000, and large screens showed the feed from CNN. The crowd cheered as battleground states such as Florida, Ohio, and Indiana were called for the hometown hero.

Then, shortly after the polls closed on the West Coast, CNN announced a projection. Most assumed that they were announcing simply that Obama would win California, Oregon and Washington, but instead they went a step further: the screens read, instead, "Barack Obama elected president."

The crowd cheered, chanted and cried, and a short while later President-elect Obama stepped to the stage in the park to address the crowd.

"If there is anyone out there who still doubts that America is a place where all things are possible," he said, "who still wonders if the dream of our founders is alive in our time; who still questions the power of our democracy, tonight is your answer."

If ever there was a night in Chicago that warranted a fifth star being added to the city flag, that was the night. Historians of the future will argue as to how successful Obama's first term was, but the American people were satisfied enough to grant him a second term in office four years later.

Obama was not only the first African American to be elected president, but one of very few modern presidents to come from an urban background. Most recent presidents had worn their small-town pride on their sleeves; indeed, throughout the election Sarah Palin's small-town background was often held up as proof that she had "American values," prompting an annoyed former Secretary of State Colin Powell to remark that he had grown up in New York, and felt that there was nothing wrong with his values. But Obama was proudly a Chicagoan, and kept his family's house on Greenwood Avenue near 50th Street, in the south side neighborhood known as Kenwood.

CHICAGO WALKING TOURS

❶ **TOUR ONE** HISTORIC SKYSCRAPERS OF THE LOOP

❷ **TOUR TWO** RIVER WALK

❸ **TOUR THREE** THEATRE DISTRICT

❹ **TOUR FOUR** LINCOLN PARK

❺ **TOUR FIVE** THOUSAND-FOOT BUILDINGS

❻ **TOUR SIX** THE MICHIGAN AVENUE CLIFF

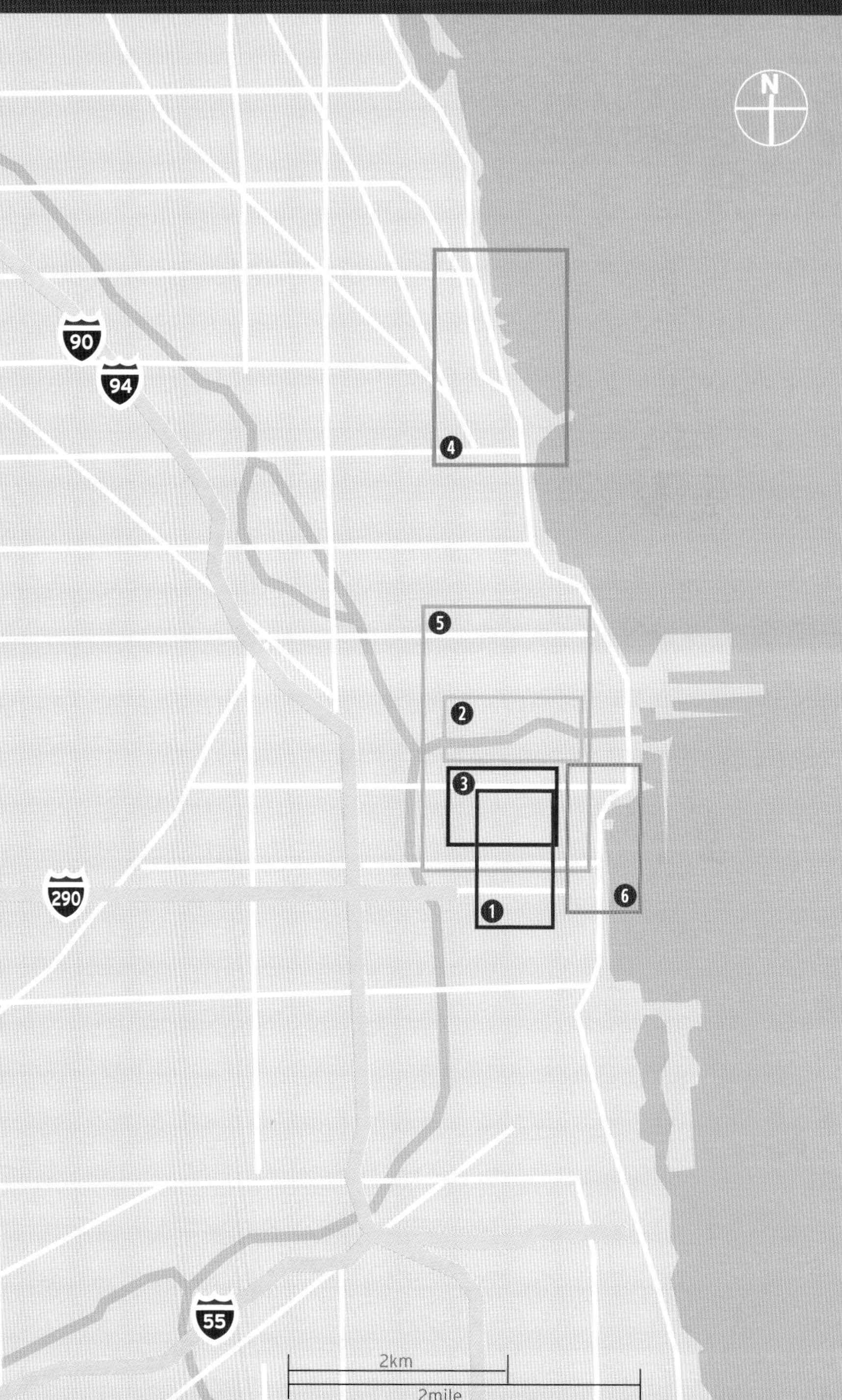

N
90
94
290
55
4
5
2
3
1
6
2km
2mile

Dearborn Street Station, between 1910 and 20

HISTORIC SKYSCRAPERS OF THE LOOP

Since the 19th century, Chicago has been synonymous with skyscrapers. Although the swampy ground made it difficult for early architects to design buildings that wouldn't sink, by the turn of the 20th century, many of the world's tallest buildings were in the Chicago Loop—thanks to ingenious advances such as the foundation structure known as the grillage, which helped keep heavy

1. Reliance Building
2. Rookery Building
3. Board of Trade Building
4. The Monadnock Building
5. The Fisher Building
6. The Old Colony Building
7. Manhattan Building
8. Old Franklin Building
9. Ellsworth Building
10. Dearborn Station

Grand
Illinois
Hubbard
Kinzie
Wells
LaSalle
Clark
Dearborn
State
Wabash
Rush
Michigan
Merchandise Mart
Chicago River
Wacker Dr.
Lake
Randolph
City Hall
Washington
Millennium Park
Madison
LOOP
Monroe
Adams
Art Institute of Chicago
Union Station
Willis Tower
Jackson
Board of Trade
Van Buren
Grant Park
PRINTERS ROW
Congress PWY
Harrison
Federal
Plymouth Ct.
Jefferson
Canal
Polk
E 8th St.
E 9th St.
Taylor
E 11th St.
400m
0.3mile
1
2
3
4
5
6
7
8
9
10

START:
Reliance Building,
1 West Washington

END:
Dearborn Station,
806 South Plymouth Ct.

Tour Time:
About 1.5 hours

structures from sinking, and the now standard balloon frame construction, in which a building is essentially plastered on to a steel skeleton, rather than having the walls support their own weight. Though many historic buildings were destroyed in the late 20th century (Chicago really lost its head in the 1970s), a great many historic skyscrapers still stand, with all of their original splendor intact.

1. Begin at 1 West Washington in the Loop, at the site of the **Reliance Building**, which is one of the earliest modern skyscrapers to survive. Built on the modern "balloon frame" model, it was among the very first skyscrapers to have windows covering a majority of the surface area. You will notice that the first floor is visibly different from the floors above it. The first floor and basement were originally designed by Burnham and Root, those great early architects of the "Chicago School," but Root died of pneumonia in 1891, while the building was still under construction. Root's plans for the rest of the building were lost, and have never been found. Charles Atwood completed the design, and the building he planned was completed in 1895. Today, the café on the ground floor bears his name, while the 122-room hotel that occupies much of the rest of the building is known as the Hotel Burnham.

Reliance Building

Daniel Burnham and John Root

Hotel Burnham

2. Walk a few blocks east to LaSalle Street and take a left (south), and you'll be walking right into the canyon of buildings that form the financial district. Proceed through the "canyon"

to 209 South LaSalle Street and take in the glorious **Rookery Building**. Built in 1888 by Burnham and Root, who installed their offices on the top floor, the 181-foot, 16-story height might not seem as impressive today, standing in the shadow of several buildings more than five times its height, but in its early days it was tall enough that from their offices, Burnham and Root could see the ongoing construction for the World's Fair in Jackson Park, several miles south. The castle-like structure is widely considered to be the firm's masterpiece. The name, taken from a building that stood on the spot before, is somewhat ironic; in the 19th century, "rookery" was a name given to ramshackle, dilapidated buildings that were filled with pigeons and rooks (crows). It was with this building, more than any other, that Burnham and Root made their statement to the world, blending exquisite ornamentation with modern techniques, including a steel frame (which was used for part of the building) and the "floating raft" grillage used in the base.

Rookery Building, 1891

"light court" at the Rookery

The centerpiece of the interior is the two-story "light court" on the inside of the entrance. In 1905, Frank Lloyd Wright redesigned the entrance in his own favored "Prairie Style."

Board of Trade building

Clock on the Rookery Building

3. Proceed south down LaSalle Street to the point at which it ends with the **Board of Trade** building at 141 West Jackson Boulevard (a 20th-century building in the midst of this walking tour full of 19th-century buildings can't simply be ignored) it has been standing at the edge of the "canyon" for the past several blocks. Designed in 1925 by Holabird and Roche, the Art Deco masterpiece stands 605 feet tall; the

Statue of Ceres

The Monadnock Building

First floor shows a thicker base

View from The Monadnock, 1890s

Dearborn Street, c. 1907

third floor has been the home of the Chicago Board of Trade for more than 80 years. The first building in town to top 600 feet in height, it was the tallest building in the city for more than 30 years after its construction, which was completed in 1930.

At the top of the building stands a 31-foot-tall aluminum statue of Ceres, the Roman goddess of grains, a reference to the commodities markets that operate inside of the building.

4. Take a left (east) on LaSalle Street and proceed to Dearborn Street. At 318 South Dearborn Street, on the corner of Dearborn Street and Jackson Boulevard, you will come across **The Monadnock Building**, which was, at the time of its construction, the tallest building in the world supporting its own weight. Also designed by Burnham and Root in 1891, just before the advent of the steel skeleton technique, the walls on the bottom level taper out to be visibly thicker at the bottom—the walls at the entrance are about six feet thick. This is only for the north half of the building; the south half is made around a steel frame (you will notice while walking past that the building changes style somewhat halfway down the block), meaning that the skyscraper really straddles two different eras of skyscraper construction. It is far less ornamental than many other 1890s skyscrapers, and evoked a few yawns when it was first designed, though later architects and critics praised it as looking forward toward the simpler designs that would dominate skyscrapers in the 20th century.

5. The Monadnock functions as the northern entrance to the Printing House Row district. Just looking south, you will see a number of notable landmarks of skyscraper construction. Walk back across the street to **343 South Dearborn** to take in the golden wonder that is **The Fisher Building**, a 20-story Neo-Gothic thing of beauty, which maintains its elegance despite being something of a hodgepodge of additions. Originally an 18-story building designed by the Burnham Company (though Charles Atwood is credited as being the real leader in the design), a couple more stories and another addition were added in 1907. The additions are easy to spot, but they blend in well with the original.

Detail of the Fisher Building

The Fisher Building

The Fisher Building, 1897

Evidence of the past

Covered in terra cotta carvings of various creatures, both real and mythical, the dominant creatures carved into the statuaries are fish, a visual shout-out to paper baron Lucius Fisher, for whom the building was first designed.

A particularly interesting feature of the interior is that, while long since converted into a residential apartment building, the doors have been left intact, so many of the doors feature frosted glass with the name of an old business on them—one of them is even the door of an old detective agency. If the security guard will let you wander the floors a bit (and they usually will, if you're polite), you will feel as though you have stepped into an old noire film from the 1940s.

6. Proceed south down Dearborn Street and cross Van Buren Street to **The Old Colony**

Old Colony Building

Manhattan Building

William Le Baron Jenney

Manhattan Building

Old Franklin Building

Building at **407 South Dearborn.** At 215 feet, the 17-story building was said to be the tallest in the city at the time of its construction in 1893-4. Built by the Holabird and Roche firm for a Boston lawyer, it was named after Plymouth Colony, and features the seal of that Massachusetts settlement around the entrances. A generation of Chicagoans knew the Old Colony as a dark-colored building, but that was merely because decades of soot had accumulated on the cream-colored stone. A massive cleaning project in recent years has restored it to its original brilliance.

7. Proceed south to **431 South Dearborn** for the last building in a cluster of historic buildings that opens Printing House Row, the **Manhattan Building**, a 16-story behemoth designed by William Le Baron Jenney. Built from 1889-91, it is the oldest surviving building in the world to be built solely upon a steel frame. The sight of a 16-story building astounded people in 1891, though today its mélange of designs makes it seem less elegant than its neighbors. But the flat windows served a purpose—when the building was built, the lower floors used curved windows in order to capture more sunlight. The windows on higher floors weren't under the shade of taller buildings nearby at the time, and didn't need to capture as much sun.

8. Continue south on Dearborn, taking in the countless Victorian skyscrapers of the old Printer's Row (and try to imagine the place as the shady area it was in the 1880s, before the skyscrapers moved in and gradually made the area more upscale). At 521-5 South Dearborn is the **Old Franklin Building**, built in 1886, and

featuring the then-novel feature of having the windows grouped closely together, providing better light for typesetters working inside.

9. Just south of Old Franklin is the **Ellsworth Building**, one of the last buildings designed by John M. Van Osdel that is still standing. Osdel opened an architectural firm in 1844, and is sometimes said to be Chicago's first architect. Built in 1892 and standing 14 stories high, the curved windows put one in mind of the Monadnock and Old Colony buildings, designed by the generation who came after Osdel.

10. Farther to the south, Dearborn Street comes to a dead end at Polk Street with the unmistakable pink granite **Dearborn Station**. Though not exactly a skyscraper in the modern sense, its 12-story central clock tower was visible from all over the city when it was completed in 1885. Originally an intercity rail station providing trains to cities such as New York and Los Angeles, carrying the famous and infamous into the city on trains with names like El Capitan and the Super Chief, the building fell out of use in the 1970s, when Amtrak moved its tracks to nearby Union Station. It was slated to be demolished for some time; in the mid 1980s it was repurposed as office and retail space, and is now the home of the Jazz Showcase, where you can see top-level jazz talent in an intimate setting.

Ellsworth Building

Dearborn Station

The El Capitan, 1967

Jazz Showcase

Chicago River east from Rush St. Bridge, c. 1905

RIVER WALK

In a remarkable feat of engineering, the flow of the Chicago River was reversed in the early 20th century, so that the city's waste and drainage would flow to the Mississippi River and down to the Gulf of Mexico, rather than into Lake Michigan. One of the most heavily engineered waterways in the world, the Chicago River is rich in history and lined with fascinating architecture.

1. The Site of Wind Blew Inn
2. Tribune Tower
3. The Wrigley Building
4. The Site of Fort Dearborn
5. McCormick Bridgehouse and Chicago River Museum
6. Trump Tower
7. Chicago Vietnam Veteran's Memorial
8. Marina City
9. United Building
10. Clark Street Bridge
11. A Plaque of The Christmas Tree Ship
12. A Plaque of *The Eastland* Disaster
13. Reid Murdoch Building
14. LaSalle Wacker Building
15. Chicago Merchandise Mart

RIVER NORTH
Ontario
Ohio
Grand
Illinois
Hubbard
Kinzie
Wells
LaSalle
Clark
Dearborn
State
Wabash
Rush
Michigan
Merchandise Mart
Chicago River
Wacker Dr.
Lake
Randolph
City Hall
Washington
Millennium Park
Madison
LOOP
Wacker Dr.
Monroe
Adams
Art Institute of Chicago
Willis Tower
Jackson
Board of Trade
Grant Park
Van Buren
Congress PWY
Harrison
400m
0.3mile
1
2
3
4
5
6
7
8
9
10
11
12
13
14
15

START:
The Site of Wind Blew Inn, Ohio Street and Michigan Avenue

END:
Chicago Merchandise Mart, 222 West Merchandise Plaza

Tour Time:
About 1.5 hours

Tribune Tower

Contest for the Tribune Tower

Brick from St. Peter's in Rome

In 2001, the city began preparing the riverfront as a pedestrian walkway, complete with green space, retail shops and eateries. The project is still ongoing, but a walk along the completed section, now known as the city's "second lakefront," is a great way to spend a summer afternoon.

1. To begin your walkway tour, start out at Ohio Street and Michigan Avenue, which was the original site of the **Wind Blew Inn**, the bohemian "tea room" operated by Lillian Collier (see Chapter 16).

2. Proceed south down Michigan Avenue towards the river, and on your left will be the magnificent Gothic skyscraper that serves as *The Chicago Tribune*'s **Tribune Tower** at 435 North Michigan Avenue, at the foot of the Magnificent Mile.

In 1922, the "Trib" held a contest for designs for its new building. Generations of architects have seen the 260 published entries as a unique way to study our changing attitudes toward what a skyscraper could and should be in the early 20th century. Though many architects were starting to veer away from the "gaudy" buildings of the 19th century and towards simpler designs by then, the winning entry was a neo-Gothic design by New Yorkers John Mead Howells and Raymond Hood. It stretched to 462 feet in height when it was completed in 1925.

The exterior of the tower is fun to explore; the lower level of the outer edge features bricks, stones, and relics from a number of important sites throughout the world. Inlaid into the stones are bits from the Pyramids; the Great Wall of China; Hamlet's Castle, Elsinore; Lincoln's Tomb; Notre Dame; and the Parthenon. There is even an actual moon rock in a glass case.

The Wrigley Building

3. Cross over Michigan Avenue to the concourse of another great Chicago icon: **The Wrigley Building** at 400 North Michigan Avenue. The gleaming, cream-colored clock tower, built in 1920 for the Wrigley Company, was one of the first major office buildings to be located north of the Chicago River, and the first in town to be air-conditioned.

Plaque marking site of the Fort

4. On the corner of Michigan Avenue and Wacker Drive, outside of the Wrigley Building, you are standing right across the river from the original site of **Fort Dearborn**, the first major settlement in the area. Fort Dearborn was a military fort that was home to roughly 100 soldiers and their families in an age when Chicago was quite literally at the edge of the wilderness. It was destroyed during the War of 1812 following a bloody battle between the soldiers, a group of Miami warriors who were helping the soldiers evacuate, and the local Potawatomi tribe. Plaques in the ground all around Wacker and Michigan mark the outline of the fort.

Entrance to River Walk

Stairs to the River Walk

McCormick Bridgehouse

5. Go down the stairs on the corner leading to the River Walk. Take a quick left, and you

Trump Tower

O'Brien's Riverwalk Cafe

Vietnam Veteran's Memorial

"Chicago Remembers"

Marina City

will find yourself at the **McCormick Bridge House and Chicago River Museum**, a museum dedicated to the river and the famous movable bridges that you will see overhead. The bridges, by the way, are still drawbridges; they are still raised up occasionally when large ships need to pass through, creating predictable headaches for traffic. The Bridgehouse Museum is open Thursday through Monday from May to October; see bridgehousemuseum.org for hours and ticket information.

6. Take a left from the stairs, and you will have a commanding view of the **Trump Tower**. Say what you will about Donald Trump (and Chicagoans say plenty about him), the building is gorgeous from this angle; on a foggy day, it looks majestic from below.

7. Proceeding along the river, you will pass by the O'Brien's Riverwalk Cafe and O'Brien's Restaurant, both of which open at 11am during tourist season.

Just beyond the two cafés, you will find yourself in Wabash Plaza, a mix of charming green space and a concourse that forms the home of the **Chicago Vietnam Veteran's Memorial**, the largest memorial to the Vietnam War outside of Washington D.C. In Wabash Plaza, the words "Chicago Remembers" appear in stone above a series of tablets, which feature the names of soldiers lost in the war.

8. From here, go back up the stairs to the corner of Wacker and State, and cross over State Street. From here on during the walking tour, you will stay at street level. Across the

river will be the "corncob" building that forms **Marina City**, a mixed-use retail and residential complex that was designed to host a "city within a city" in its twin 65-story, 578-foot towers. Designed by Bertrand Goldberg in 1959, by the time of the towers' completion in 1964, they were sometimes said to be the most photographed buildings in the world, and were the tallest residential buildings in the world for a few years until the Hancock Building shattered the record. Built of reinforced concrete, they feature a gym, bowling alley, radio station, grocery store, and several other amenities for the residents. The 20th floor of each building features laundry rooms that have, perhaps, the best view of any laundry facility in the world. Many of the facilities within fell into disuse over the years; the movie theater was not used for ages before it was turned into the new House of Blues.

House of Blues

The Hunter, 1980

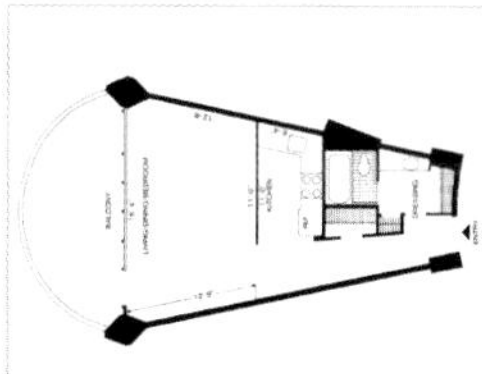
Apartment layout

United Building

The towers have been seen in several movies and TV shows, including the introduction to *The Bob Newhart Show* (it was widely thought that Newhart's character lived in the towers) and the 1980 film *The Hunter*, in which a character drives out of the parking area and falls into the river below.

The wedge-shaped apartments within are still surprisingly affordable, though modern residents complain that the concrete structure makes for lousy cell phone reception.

9. Proceed west along the river and cross over Dearborn Street. On your left will be the post-modern **United Building** at 77 West Wacker Drive. Built as a sort of post-modern take on the

Clark Street Bridge

Clark Street Bridge, c. 1900

Vinnie "The Schemer" Drucci

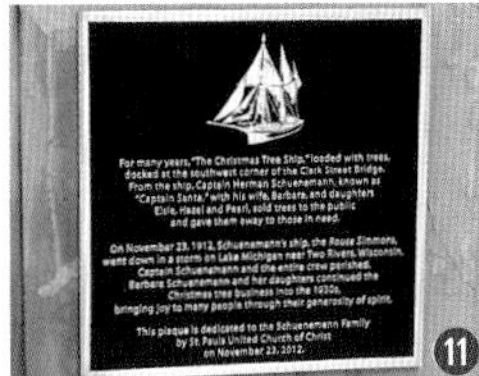

Plaque for The Christmas Tree Ship

The Christmas Tree Ship

"glass boxes" that had dominated skyscraper construction for years when it was built in 1992, many saw it as a welcome step away from the "less is more" school of architecture pioneered by Mies van der Rohe, particularly those counter the "less is more" motto with "less is a bore."

10. Cross **Clark Street** over the bridge. The bridge itself is rich in history; an earlier version was the site of the Lager Beer Riots of 1856, when angry citizens rioted against mayor Levi Boone's plans to close German beer halls on Sunday (Boone was a member of the anti-immigrant Know Nothing Party, which was briefly popular in the 1850s). Decades later in 1927, gangster Vinnie "The Schemer" Drucci was killed on the bridge. Known as perhaps the wildest and most inventive gangster on the North Side in the Prohibition era, Drucci got his name by coming up with wild schemes and heists for the gang, such as a plan to go to London and steal the crown jewels. Though the gang talked him out of a plan to run for mayor in 1927, he remained active in the mayoral race, and when the local election day came around in that year, gangsters were going around kidnapping people who worked for, or just planned to vote for, their chosen candidate's opponents. Drucci was rounded up by the police, and was shot to death on the bridge when he tried to grab for an officer's gun.

11. Proceeding along when you've crossed over Clark along the river, you will first come to a new plaque marking the spot where a generation of Chicagoans would gather to await the arrival of *The Rouse Simmons*, known

throughout the city as "The Christmas Tree Ship," which would arrive on this spot loaded with Christmas trees from Wisconsin and Michigan to sell to Chicagoans. It would arrive decked in Christmas lights (still a novelty in the first decade of the 20th century) and with a Christmas tree tied to the top mast, and piloted by Herman Schuenemann, who was known as "Captain Santa."

However, in November of 1912, during a Christmas tree shortage, Captain Santa overloaded the ship with 5,500 trees, far more than it could safely carry. Storm winds began to blow in as the ship sailed through the lakes towards Chicago, and four ships, including *The Rouse Simmons*, were lost in the storm that night. The wreckage—which still contained some trees—was discovered in 1971.

12. Only a few steps down along the river is a marker for an even more tragic story—*The Eastland* Disaster. In July of 1915, the steamship *S.S. Eastland* capsized here in the river due to a mixture of mechanical problems, poor design, and overcrowding (workers on the ship had recently decided that having enough life boats for 2,500 people meant that they could raise their capacity from 2,200 to 2,500). A total of 844 people, including 22 entire families, who had come for the Western Electric company's annual excursion to Michigan City, Indiana, lost their lives that day.

13. Across the river, one can see the **Reid Murdoch Building**, the large red building with a clock tower in the middle, which served as a hospital after the tragedy.

"Captain Santa"

The *Eastland* Disaster, 1915

Scene from the disaster

Reid Murdoch Building

The Eastland Disaster Plaque

LaSalle Wacker Building

Frank "The Enforcer" Nitti (center)

LaSalle Street Bridge

LaSalle Street Bridge

LaSalle St. Bridge, looking south

At a glance, the clock tower appears to be right in the center of the Reid Murdoch building. Look a little closer, though, and you will see that it is actually off-center; the portion of the building on the right is larger than the portion on the left. It was right in the center when the building was first constructed, but a portion of it on the left was torn down when LaSalle Street was expanded.

At the corner of LaSalle Street and Wacker Drive is a plaque commemorating *The Eastland disaster.*

14. Across the street, on the other side of Wacker, is the armchair-shaped **LaSalle Wacker Building**. Designed by Holabird and Root and built in 1930, the 41-story tall structure was briefly the headquarters of the Capone Gang after Capone was sent to prison and Frank "The Enforcer" Nitti took over control of the group; a police raid on their office in the building very nearly cost Nitti his life, and some say that the subsequent assassination of Mayor Cermak (officially an accident; the shooter was said to be aiming for President-elect Franklin D. Roosevelt) was actually a very-much intentional retaliation for Cermak's attempts to crack down on gang activity.

15. Cross over the river on the LaSalle Street Bridge (enter the western lobby of the Reid Murdoch building to see a collection of photographs from *The Eastland* Disaster), then cross over LaSalle Street and proceed along the river until you cross Wells Street, and you will soon find yourself in the concourse of the **Chicago Merchandise Mart**, at 222

West Merchandise Mart Plaza. Built in 1930, at the time of its construction it was the largest (though not the tallest) building in the world, including four million square feet. So large was the building that when ZIP codes were introduced in 1963, the Merchandise Mart had one all to itself.

Chicago Merchandise Mart

Originally owned by the family of Marshall Field, and then by the Kennedy family (yes, *that* Kennedy family), the concourse area outside features several pillars topped by busts, resembling gigantic PEZ dispensers. These are busts of various giants of merchandising, including Marshall Field, Montgomery Ward, Frank Woolworth and Edward Filene.

Busts of giants of merchandising

The inside of the building is not the great shopping experience one would think; much of the space is given over to wholesale warehousing. However, the lower levels are home to a massive Luxe Home store, and the second floor features several retail shops and a food court, as well as an entrance to a Brown Line L track, from which you can hop a train to explore more of the city around the Loop and the North Side.

View from the Mart, c. 1941

View from the Mart

In front of the movie theater, 1941

THEATRE DISTRICT

The main theater district in the Loop is home to several gorgeous theaters, many dating back to the early 20th century, hosting everything from concerts and lectures to touring productions of Broadway hits. Although New York's Broadway might remain the premiere venue for American theater, many of the biggest Broadway hits open for previews in Chicago before moving to New York,

❶ Chicago Theatre
❷ Oriental Theatre
❸ The Goodman Theatre
❹ Cadillac Palace Theatre
❺ Chicago Temple
❻ Bank of America Theatre

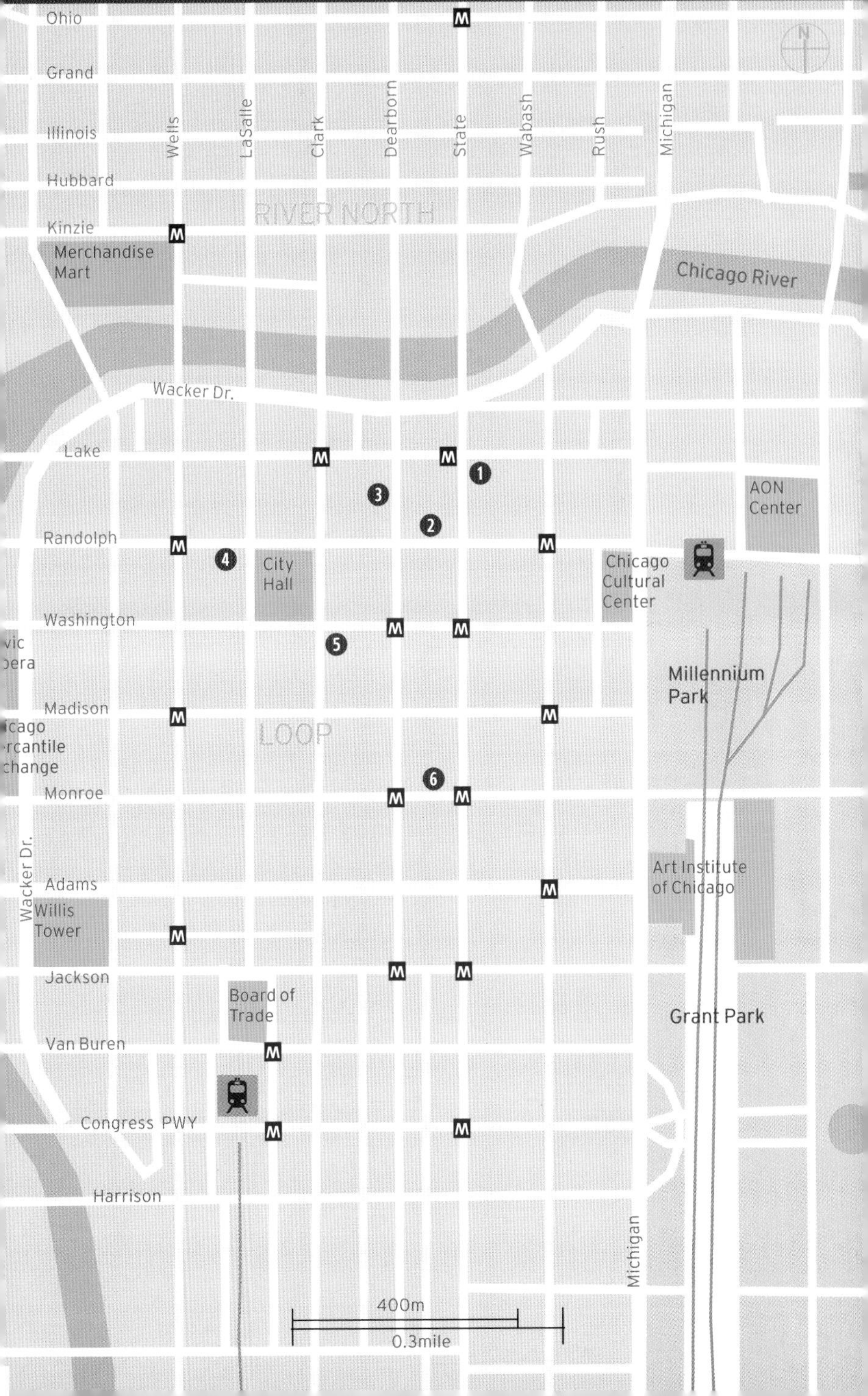

Ohio
Grand
Illinois
Hubbard
Kinzie
Wells
LaSalle
Clark
Dearborn
State
Wabash
Rush
Michigan
RIVER NORTH
Merchandise Mart
Chicago River
Wacker Dr.
Lake
1
3
2
AON Center
Randolph
4
City Hall
Chicago Cultural Center
Washington
5
Millennium Park
Madison
LOOP
6
Monroe
Wacker Dr.
Adams
Art Institute of Chicago
Willis Tower
Jackson
Board of Trade
Grant Park
Van Buren
Congress PWY
Harrison
Michigan
400m
0.3mile

START:
Chicago Theatre, State Street and Lake Street

END:
Bank of America Theatre, 18 West Monroe Street

Tour Time:
About 1.5 hours

giving Chicagoans a chance to see the new shows before New Yorkers do.

In the 1920s, the Loop was filled with movie palaces and vaudeville houses, some of which dated back decades. On Madison Street, a pre-Fire version of McVicker's Theater had hosted John Wilkes Booth in a three-week run in which he played several of the greatest Shakespeare roles. At Clark and Madison stood the venerable Clark Theater, which was open for 23 hours per day, showing a different double feature every night.

The great majority of these theaters were gone by 1990, but a number of beautiful theaters are still in operation.

Chicago Theatre

Chicago Theatre, 1949

Entertainment Magazine covers by Balaban and Katz

1. Start at State Street and Lake Street, home of the famous **Chicago Theatre**. Built in 1921, shots of the theater's famous marquee are frequently shown in movies to make viewers think that a movie taking place in Chicago was actually shot there (although the marquee shot might be the only one that wasn't shot in Toronto, where many Chicago movies are filmed). Originally opened as a silent movie theater by the venerable Balaban and Katz company, the lavish interior is almost *too* gaudy by today's standards. Opening in 1921, it featured its own orchestra, a Wurlitzer organ, and live stage shows in addition to the movie (the feature on opening day was *The Sign on the Door*).

The fortunes of the theater rose and fell over the years; stage shows were discontinued in the 1950s, and the theater closed altogether in 1985, by which time single-screen movie theaters were an anachronism, re-opening a year later as a concert venue, which it continues to be today. It is hard to imagine seeing a movie in the lavish French Baroque interior, but this drives home just how much we have lost from the movie-going experience in the multiplex era. Tours of the venue are available most days; typically at noon from Sunday through Friday, and at 11am and 12:30pm on Saturdays.

Lavish interior of Oriental

2. Proceed one block south down State Street, turn right on Randolph Street and cross State Street towards the **Oriental Theatre**. Standing on the site of the Iroquois Theatre, where a 1903 fire killed around 600 people (though only one foundation-level wall remains), the Oriental opened in 1926, when it functioned primarily as a vaudeville house. Over the next few decades, it hosted a veritable who's who of 20th century entertainers, including Bob Hope, the Three Stooges, Billie Holiday and the Marx Brothers. Inside of the theater, employees recently moved a piece of paper that was pinned to a backstage wall and found lipstick prints, signed and dated from the 1930s on the wall. The signatures and prints are believed to be those of a dancing troupe called The Dancing Sweethearts that was appearing at the theater the week the prints are dated.

Iroquois Theatre, 1902

Tragic fire in 1903

Oriental Theatre, 1926

By the 1970s, the theater had fallen on hard times, and stayed in business mainly by showing Kung Fu movies. It was deserted and thought to be lost forever throughout

Oriental Theatre, now the Ford

Wicked at the Oriental Theatre

The Goodman Theatre

Del Close

Cadillac Palace Theatre

the 1980s, then was extensively restored and re-opened as a theater venue in 1998 under the name Ford Center for the Performing Arts Oriental Theatre. Today, it hosts touring and preview productions of major Broadway shows, including a three-and-a-half year run of *Wicked.* Tours of the theater are often run on Saturdays.

3. Proceed one block south to Dearborn Street. Across the street and half a block north, you will see **The Goodman Theatre**, a complex of several small theaters that host The Goodman, the oldest currently active nonprofit theater company in the city. A skull said to be that of comedian Del Close, who donated his skull to the theater so that he could play Yorick in *Hamlet*, is in a glass case in the artistic director's office, though the theater is pretty open about the fact that it wasn't Del's skull when he was alive.

4. Proceed down Randolph Street past Clark Street to the **Cadillac Palace Theatre**, just west of LaSalle Street at 151 West Randolph. Opened in 1926 under the name The New Palace Theatre, the architecture was designed by George and Cornelius Rapp, the same brothers who designed the nearby Oriental Theatre. The interior was designed to look like a French palace, and was inspired by such palaces as Versailles and the Fontainebleau. Originally opened as a vaudeville house, interest in vaudeville was already on the wane in 1926, and only five years later it was converted into a movie theater. In the 1980s, it was briefly renamed the Bismarck and functioned as a concert venue.

Cadillac purchased the naming rights to the venue in 1999 and re-opened it as the Cadillac Palace, which plays host to touring Broadway shows and pre-Broadway previews of the next hits, including the original preview run of the Tony Award-winning *The Producers* with Matthew Broderick (only blocks from the sites where he had played Ferris Bueller a decade and a half before).

5. Return to LaSalle Street and take a right, then turn left on Washington Street back to Clark, where you can't fail to see the steeple of the **Chicago Temple** at 77 West Washington, which functions both as a church and a theater. Built in 1924, at 568 feet tall, it was the tallest building in Chicago until the Board of Trade building opened in 1930, and is still sometimes said to be the tallest church building in the world. The Neo-Gothic tower houses three sanctuaries, including a tiny "sky chapel" at the base of the steeple, built using money from the Walgreen family in 1952.

In addition to functioning as the First Methodist Church, the building is home to Silk Road Rising, a theater group that shows theatrical works by Asian and Middle-Eastern authors. Originally known as the Silk Road Theater Project, Silk Road Rising became a theater-in-residence in the Temple Building in 2003, utilizing the 99-seat Pierce Theater space on the lower level as a permanent performance space. In the space is the stunning mural, *The Silk Road*, a gift to Silk Road Rising from world-renowned artists The Zhou Brothers.

Cadillac Palace Theatre interior

New Palace Theatre, c. 1926-29

New Palace Theatre, 1956

Chicago Temple building

Rumi by Silk Road Rising

Bank of America Theatre

Harry Houdini (center)

Majestic Theatre Bar, c. 1910

Shubert Theatre, 1966

6. Head south on Clark Street and take a left on Monroe Street, and you will see the **Bank of America Theatre** at 18 West Monroe. Older than most other theaters in the district, the venue originally opened as The Majestic Theatre, a vaudeville house that offered several acts per day, running from the early afternoon through late at night. Harry Houdini was among the countless famous headliners who performed in the venue during its first 25 years. Like the Oriental and the Palace, the interiors were designed by the Rapp Brothers, with the aid of Edmund Kraus, using bright colors to attract more upper-class patrons than other vaudeville houses.

The Great Depression hit the theater district hard, and the Majestic was closed in 1932, remaining shut until 1945, when it became the Shubert Theatre. It became the LaSalle Bank Theatre in 2006, and then became the Bank of America Theatre when the LaSalle Bank Corporation was purchased by Bank of America two years later.

Today, the theater is part of the Broadway in Chicago Organization, and hosted a long run of *The Book of Mormon,* which some believe will run for years. *Jersey Boys* ran at the theater for more than two years beginning in 2007, and in 2004 the theater hosted the pre-Broadway previews of *Monty Python's Spamalot,* starring Tim Curry, David Hyde Pierce and Hank Azaria.

OLD CHICAGO SCENE: Seeing Chicago, auto at Monroe near State, between 1900 and 1915

Around a bubbling cup, Lincoln Park, 1910-20

LINCOLN PARK

Stretching up the north side of the city along Lake Michigan, Lincoln Park is one of Chicago's finest green spaces. Officially stretching for 11 miles from Ohio Street to Ardmore Avenue, and featuring a bike trail that makes it easy to travel the whole of the park, for this walking tour we will focus on a walkable area between North Avenue and Fullerton Parkway (which becomes Fullerton Avenue farther west).

1. Chicago History Museum
2. Statue of Abraham Lincoln
3. Couch Tomb
4. Benjamin Franklin Monument
5. Green City Market
6. Lincoln Park Farm-in-the-Zoo
7. Burial site of David Kennison
8. Lincoln Park Zoo
9. Lincoln Park Conservatory
10. Site of the St. Valentine's Day Massacre

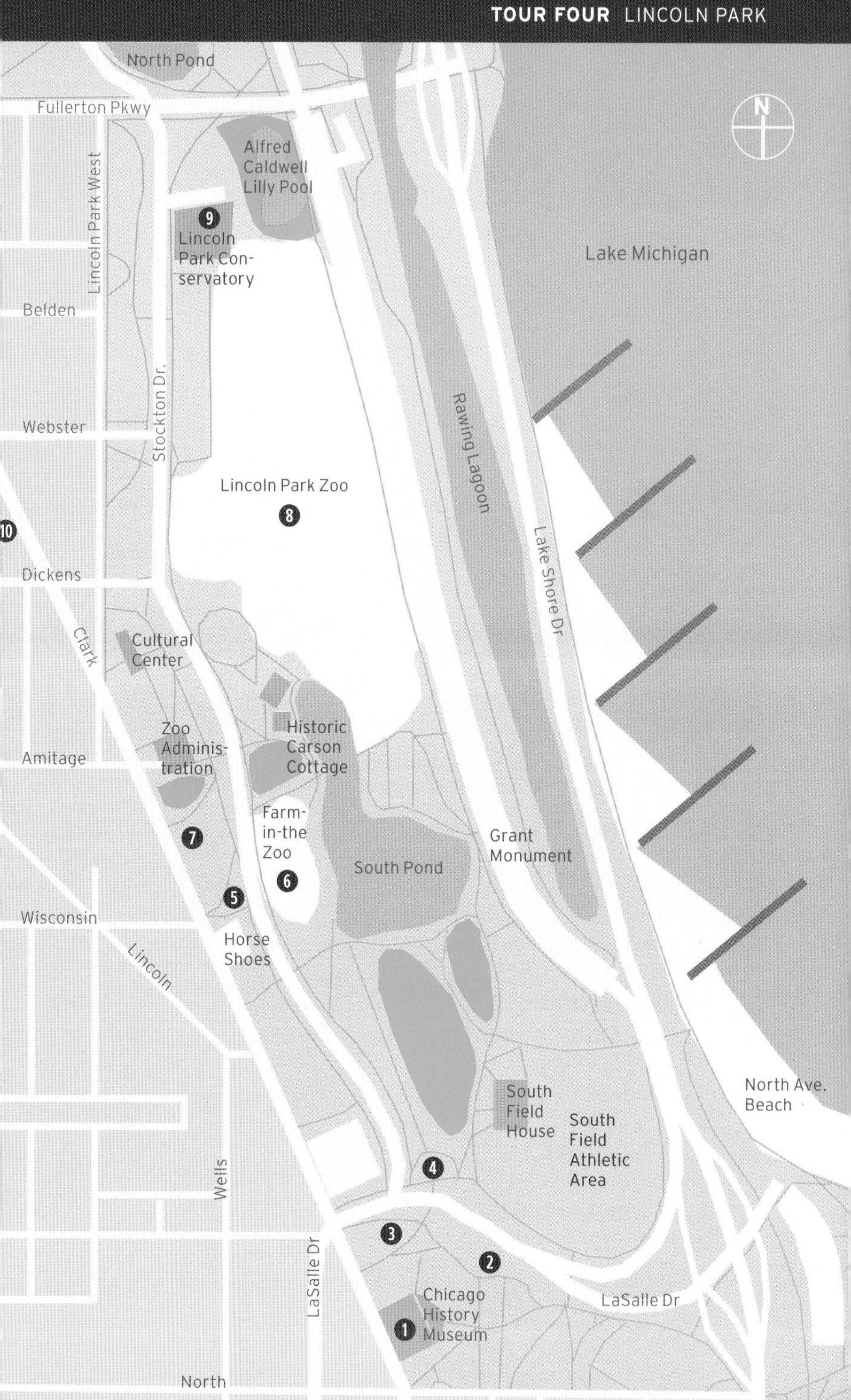
North Pond
Fullerton Pkwy
Alfred Caldwell Lilly Pool
N
Lincoln Park West
9
Lincoln Park Conservatory
Lake Michigan
Belden
Stockton Dr.
Rawing Lagoon
Webster
Lincoln Park Zoo
8
10
Lake Shore Dr
Dickens
Clark
Cultural Center
Zoo Administration
Historic Carson Cottage
Amitage
Farm-in-the Zoo
Grant Monument
7
South Pond
5
6
Wisconsin
Horse Shoes
Lincoln
South Field House
South Field Athletic Area
North Ave. Beach
Wells
4
3
LaSalle Dr
2
Chicago History Museum
1
LaSalle Dr
North

START:
Chicago History Museum, 1601 North Clark Street

END:
The Site of St. Valentine's Day Massacre

Tour Time:
About 3 hours

The land for the park was originally set aside by the city in the 1840s as grounds for a City Cemetery—a very progressive move in an age when most who died in large cities were buried in churchyards that became overcrowded very quickly, leading to poor sanitary conditions. At the time, the land that would become the park was far out in the outskirts of the city. However, over the next two decades, the city kept expanding northwards, and around the end of the Civil War a decision was made to remove the bodies and turn the land into a park. It was soon named "Lincoln Park" after the recently assassinated President Lincoln.

Chicago History Museum

East façade of museum

The Great Fire diorama

1. Begin at the south end of this portion of the park, outside of the **Chicago History Museum** at 1601 North Clark Street. If you wish to stop inside, the museum features several fascinating exhibits, including the bed on which Abraham Lincoln died.

Walk around the back of the museum into the concourse area behind it, where a semicircular seating area is surrounded by bushes. Explore the bushes and you will find some fascinating artifacts. One is a large chain, said to have been used to block British ships traversing through New England rivers during the Revolutionary War (though the museum is quite open about the fact that the provenance of the chains is fairly shaky; it's one of a number of dubious Revolutionary War relics in the collection). Elsewhere among the bushes is a huge chunk of metal that was all that remained of an early Chicago department store after the Great Chicago Fire.

2. Proceed a little to the east and you will come to the concourse leading up to the life-sized **statue of Abraham Lincoln** that was built by renowned sculptor Augustus Saint-Gaudens. Built using a life-mask taken of Lincoln during his lifetime, it has become one of the best-known of the many, many statues of Lincoln throughout the world; thousands, including many of Lincoln's own friends and relatives, attended the dedication ceremony in 1887.

3. Backtrack to the west and you will see a strange little stone building surrounded by a low metal fence. This is the last major relic of the space's time as City Cemetery, the **Couch Family Mausoleum**. Built in 1858 to house the remains of Ira Couch, a hotel owner (whose Tremont House Hotel on Lake and Dearborn Streets hosted both Abraham Lincoln and John Wilkes Booth at various times), the massive tomb was left on the grounds after the rest of the cemetery was moved for reasons that are not exactly known (most likely, the city simply didn't want to spend the $3,000 it would have cost them to move the structure). Opinions differ on whether there are still any bodies interred in the tomb; as of a century ago, Couch's grandson told a Chicago newspaper that he believed that there were about eight people inside, though even then, no one seemed to be entirely sure, and it has not been opened in well over a hundred years. Thousands of Chicagoans drive right past the tomb every day without realizing what it is.

Statue of Abraham Lincoln

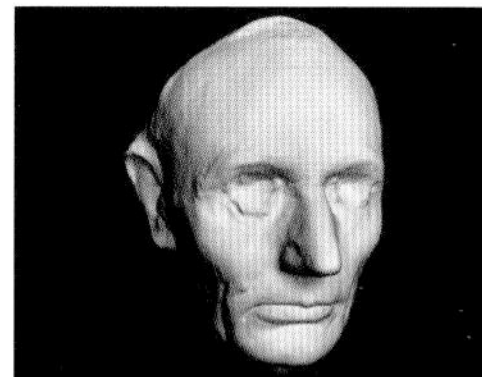
Life mask of Lincoln

Couch Family Mausoleum

Mausoleum, 1903

Ira Couch

Benjamin Franklin Monument

Green City Market

Green City Market stalls

Lincoln Park Farm-in-the-Zoo

Barns at the Farm-in-the-Zoo

Although the Couch tomb is the last major relic of the cemetery today (above the ground, at least), the transition from cemetery to park was a gradual one, and many tombs were still visible for decades after the cemetery was closed (one was used as a tool shed for a while). At the time of the Great Chicago Fire in 1871, the park/cemetery area was as far north as the fire got, and there were stories of people taking shelter in recently excavated graves; the tomb is now the oldest structure still standing in the Chicago fire zone.

4. From the tomb, walk down the hill on the bike path, and proceed north through the tunnel beneath LaSalle Drive, and you will find yourself right at the feet of the **Benjamin Franklin Monument**. Originally built for the 1893 World's Fair by Richard Henry Park, the statue was installed in Lincoln Park three years later, originally near the south lagoon farther to the north.

5. Go around the left-hand side of the statue and there are two paths leading north. The path on the right, directly behind Franklin, will take you up towards the South Pond, through the space where **Green City Market**, one of the city's largest farmer's markets, is held in spring, summer and fall months on Wednesday and Saturday mornings.

6. The left-hand path will take you right to the gates of the **Lincoln Park Farm-in-the-Zoo**, an out-cropping of the nearby Lincoln Park Zoo featuring farm animals such as sheep, goats, chickens, and other animals that city kids are not exposed to often. The petting zoo and main

barn feature attractions suitable for all ages.

7. Across Stockton Drive (which cuts through the park) from the Farm-in-the-Zoo is one of the more interesting monuments in the park; a boulder marking the approximate **burial site of David Kennison**. At the time of his death in 1855, Kennison was telling everyone in town that he was 115 years old, and the last surviving participant of the Boston Tea Party. He was buried with full military honors, but his was one of the bodies left behind when the cemetery was moved, and several decades later, a group of elderly Chicagoans who remembered the funeral got together and pinpointed the site of the boulder as his burial place, and the marker was placed on the spot.

There are a couple of problems with this site, though. For one thing, Pamela Bannos, the city's expert on City Cemetery, believes that they weren't even close to right when they determined that this site was his burial place; he was probably actually buried near the Couch tomb a couple of blocks south. For another, it's now known that Kennison wasn't telling the truth about his age or war record—he was about 30 years younger than he claimed to be. Even a quick fact-check of his various war stories would have told people that he claimed to have been a prisoner-of-war in New York at the same time as Cornwallis's surrender at Yorktown, which he also claimed to have attended, and he couldn't have possibly been in both places at once. Still, the History Museum still has some tea leaves that he said were from Boston—another of the Revolutionary War relics that they are happy to admit are of dubious origin!

Burial site of David Kennison

Plaque on Kennison's grave

David Kennison

Lincoln Park Zoo

City views from the park

Lincoln Park Zoo, 1912

Lincoln Park Conservatory

Al Capone

8. Proceed north and you will come to the main **Lincoln Park Zoo** on the right-hand side. The zoo has everything one would expect from such a zoo: lions, tigers, rhinos, giraffes, apes and everything in between. One can easily spend an entire day there. And here's the best part: it's free. You can walk right in from the park!

9. Proceed farther north through the park and you will come to the massive **Lincoln Park Conservatory**, a botanical garden at 2391 North Stockton Drive. A greenhouse has operated on this site since the 1870s, when the park was brand new, and the conservatory now on the site was built in the 1890s. The grounds nearby feature monuments to Friedrich Schiller (a German poet) and William Shakespeare, as well as a fountain that was installed in 1886. These surrounding gardens are among the oldest gardens in the city. Inside, a portion of the conservatory is free, and is described by the park district as "Paradise Under Glass," featuring tens of thousands of plant species.

10. Proceed just north to Fullerton Parkway for a detour many Chicago tourists want to take. Take a left on Fullerton and walk two blocks down the road to Clark Street, and cross onto the west side of Clark. Take a left, and you will pass a senior apartment complex. Just beyond this, you will see a little field and parking area behind a gate. This was the site of the **St. Valentine's Day Massacre**. In this field stood the SMC Cartage Company, where seven men affiliated with the Bugs Moran gang were shot by members of the Al Capone Gang on Valentine's Day, 1929. A tree in the middle used to mark the site of the North Wall, where

the men were lined up, but it was cut down in 2013. To get a sense of where the garage was, look out into the field and notice the part where the grassy area extends further back; the north wall was a couple of feet to the right. No plaque marks the spot today; rumor has it that Richard J. Daley wanted the building torn down when he was the mayor to curb Chicago's reputation as "the Gangster City." A lot of good it did him; even now, gangster stories are turning up in walking tours of parks!

Site of Valentine's Day massacre

SMC Cartage Company, 1929

The Heart of Chicago, c. 1900 or 1901

THOUSAND-FOOT BUILDINGS

Although Chicago didn't have a building more than 600 feet tall until 1930, today it is home to dozens of tall buildings; as of 2013, there are more than 40 buildings over the 600 foot mark, and another 40 that stand more than 500. Five Chicago buildings now claim the title of "super skyscraper," a term given to buildings that stretch past the 1,000-foot mark.

1. John Hancock Building
2. Trump International Hotel
3. Aon Center
4. Two Prudential Plaza
5. The Franklin Center
6. Willis Tower
7. 311 South Wacker Drive

COALD COAST
Newberry Library
Washington Square
Rush
Oak
Walton
Delaware
Chestnut
Peason
John Hancock Center
Water Tower
Museum of Contemp. Art
Chicago Ave.
Superior
Huron
Erie
Wells
LaSalle
Clark
Dearborn
State
Wabash
Rush
The Magnificent Mile
Lake Shore Dr
Ontario
Ohio
Michigan
STREETERVILLE
Grand
Illinois
Hubbard
Kinzie
RIVER NORTH
Columbus Dr.
N. Water
Merchandise Mart
Carroll
Chicago River
Wacker Dr.
S. Water
Lake
Randolph
City Hall
Washington
Millennium Park
Madison
Wacker Dr.
LOOP
Monroe
PRINTERS ROW
Adams
Willis Tower
Art Institute of Chicago
Jackson
Board of Trade
Lake Michigan
Van Buren
Grant Park
Congress PWY
Federal
Plymouth Ct.
Harrison
LaSalle
Clark
Dearborn
State
Wabash
Michigan
Lake Shore Dr
Polk
E 8th St.
Wells
400m
0.3mile

START:
John Hancock Building
875 North Michigan Avenue

END:
311 South Wacker Drive

Tour Time:
About 2 hours

Chicago was not the first city to have such a building—Paris beat it to the punch with the Eiffel Tower in the 1880s, and New York's Empire State Building reached 1,250 feet in 1931. However, no city has quite so many super skyscrapers as Chicago, and all of them can be seen in a walking tour that takes you roughly one mile from the Magnificent Mile to the southern portion of the Loop.

Chicago skyline

John Hancock Building

John Hancock construction site, 1966

1. Begin at **875 North Michigan Avenue** with the **John Hancock Building**, the first of Chicago's skyscrapers to reach the thousand-foot mark (and the farthest to the north). Built in 1968, at the time of its construction the massive trapezoid-shaped building was the tallest in the world (outside of New York City), and featured the highest residential real estate anywhere (the condos towards the top of the building are still among the highest-from-the-ground residential real estate to be found anywhere). A lobby on the 44th floor has the world's highest indoor swimming pool; the skating rink that operates for part of the year in the observatory level is the world's highest skating rink.

Among locals, it's generally said that the view from the observatory level is better than the view from the somewhat taller Willis Tower, though if you wish to skip the lines and the fees for the observatory, simply go to the Signature Room on the 95th floor for a cocktail. The

Hancock Building is now the fourth tallest in Chicago.

The Hancock Building is a part of the area still known to Chicagoans as Streeterville, in honor of Captain George Wellington Streeter, who claimed ownership of the landfill on the grounds in the 1880s, and then declared it to be an independent country, leading to a 30-year battle between the city and "Cap" Streeter and his army of hobos. It is hard to imagine, looking at the area that includes such landmarks as the Drake Hotel and the Water Tower Place shopping center, that it was a "shanty town" so recently.

2. From the Hancock Building, walk south down the Magnificent Mile. As you cross the Michigan Avenue Bridge over the Chicago River, you will be treated to a view of the sparkling silver **Trump International Hotel**. It stands on the site of the former offices of the *Chicago Sun Times* (which were located in a hideous seven-story glass building that few were sad to see demolished). When Donald Trump announced his plans for the building in July of 2001, he intended for the building to reach a height of 1,500 feet, which would have made it the tallest building in the world. Such a height would still have made it the tallest in Chicago today (though overseas buildings have towered well beyond that mark in the past few years and would have left it in the dust internationally). After the terrorist attacks on September 11, 2001, Trump decided that such a building would be a safety risk and scaled back his plans. He initially unveiled a design for a 1,073-foot building in December of 2001, but

Night view from John Hancock

Trump International Hotel

Chicago Sun Times building, 2003

Donald Trump

Trump International Hotel

Interior, Trump International Hotel

Trump International Hotel

The Waterview Tower

The Waterview Tower, 2013

Chicago Spire (rendering)

the original bland, bulky design was met with wide disapproval. After a series of revisions and a dispute with the mayor (who wanted the building to have a spire, a development at which Trump balked), construction on the building finally began in 2005, and, when completed, the building topped out at 1,170 feet (or 1,389, if you count the spire), with residences slightly higher than those in the Hancock Building. Many Chicagoans hope that the building will eventually get a new name, and some who dislike Trump refer to it as the "Donald Duck Building."

From the bridge, you are also within sight of a couple of planned super skyscapers that never made it. The Waterview Tower at 111 West Wacker Drive was originally planned to be just over a thousand feet tall. Almost unknown around the city (only in Chicago could there be a 1,000-foot building under construction that no one knew about), the construction ceased in 2008 due to funding problems, and sat as a small, unfinished skeleton for years. In 2012, a new company took over to complete the building, though it is now planned only to go up to around 600 feet.

Even less fortunate was the planned Chicago Spire that was to be built on Lake Shore Drive. Planned as a sort of twisting corkscrew design that would reach 2,000 feet in height, construction was abandoned after the foundation was made, leaving Chicago with what appears to be a bottomless pit. Today the site is buried under various lawsuits and debts, but a recent re-emergence of interest has sparked hopes among some Chicagoans that the Spire might yet be built, after all, although any new developer who takes on the site is likely to scale the plans back from the initial 2,000-foot structure.

3. Continue down Michigan Avenue to Randolph Street and take a left (east) to the **Aon Center** at 200 East Randolph Street, currently Chicago's third-tallest building at 1,136 feet. Originally built in 1974 as the Standard Oil Building, it was known in the city as "Big Stan," a neighbor of "Big John" (the Hancock building), and was the tallest building in Chicago for roughly a year before the Sears Tower was completed. Built from 43,000 slabs of Italian marble, it was the tallest marble building in the world at the time, though much of it has since been resurfaced with granite, because the marble turned out to be terribly unstable.

In 1985, the building was sold and became The Amoco Building, giving it the distinction of being the tallest building in the world ever to undergo a name change at the time. It changed names again, to its current name of the Aon Center, in 1999.

4. Directly east of the Aon Center at 180 North Stetson Avenue stands **Two Prudential Plaza**, which at 995 feet misses the distinction of being a super skyscraper by only five feet. No other skyscraper in the world comes so close to 1,000 feet without going over the line; one wonders why they did not simply duct tape a couple of yardsticks onto the top of the spire when the building was completed in 1990.

Aon Center

Aon Center

Two Prudential Plaza

From Millennium Park

The Franklin Center

Entrance to the Franklin Center

Willis Tower

Entrance of the Willis Tower

Willis Tower

5. Go back to Michigan Avenue and continue south (perhaps taking in the Michigan Avenue Cliff, much of which separates the Aon from the next super skyscaper to the south), then take a right (west) on Monroe Street, proceeding to 227 West Monroe Street, the site of **The Franklin Center**, which stands 1,007 feet tall and 60 stories high. Originally built as the AT&T building in 1989, the vaguely Art Deco design makes it fit in well with its neighbor, the Board of Trade Building built in 1930. Although it is certainly overshadowed as a tourist attraction by some of its more famous neighbors, the Art Deco interiors are still stunning.

6. Proceed two blocks east down Monroe Street and Franklin Street, and you will find yourself at the most famous Chicago skyscraper of them all,**Willis Tower**, whose official address is 233 South Wacker Drive, and which, despite its 2009 name change, Chicagoans still refer to as the Sears Tower. The height of the building is variously given as between 1,450 and 1,455 feet tall, because the building was built on a hill, and the height depends on where along the hill you start measuring. Whatever the exact number, it held the rank of the tallest building in the world for more than 25 years, and held onto the title of "tallest occupied floor" for a few years after that, as the first buildings that soared past it in height only did so by having spires that pushed them over the 1,450 mark (Willis Tower antennas are not counted towards its height; if they did, the building would be listed as 1,729 feet high). It is now the

second tallest in the country (after New York's new Freedom Tower) and the eighth-tallest free-standing structure in the world.

View from the Sky Box

Opened in 1973 using the revolutionary "tube bundle" style, the tower is still instantly recognizable, and visible from far away on the interstate. From the Skydeck, visitors can see four states on a clear day (Wisconsin, Illinois, Indiana, and, on really clear days, Michigan). The recently added glass-bottom "sky boxes" give visitors a chance to see directly below them to the ground, which is more than 1,350 feet below. The entrance for tourists is along the Jackson Street side of the building; lines can be very long, and some locals suggest the Hancock Building observatory (or the Signature Room) as a good alternative, though the Hancock lacks the sky boxes.

View from the Willis Tower

View from Willis Tower

The name of the tower was changed in 2009 when the Willis Company took over the building (Sears' naming rights expired in 2003), though the Willis Company at least cancelled their ill-advised plans to help rebrand the building by painting it silver. Chicagoans are still known to fix anyone who calls itWillis Tower with a dirty look.

View from Willis tower

7. Just a few blocks south stands **311 South Wacker Drive**, which at 961 feet is the tallest building in the world that doesn't have a name of its own. Built in 1990 and sometimes referred to as "The White Castle" or the "Ring Building," it is easily spotted in the skyline by its glowing 100 foot cylindrical "crown." It is surrounded by

311 South Wacker Drive

311 South Wacker Drive

a park, which forms the largest green space in the Loop. There is no observation deck, but the 46th floor has a gorgeous "sky lobby" that hosts wedding receptions, meetings and other such get-togethers.

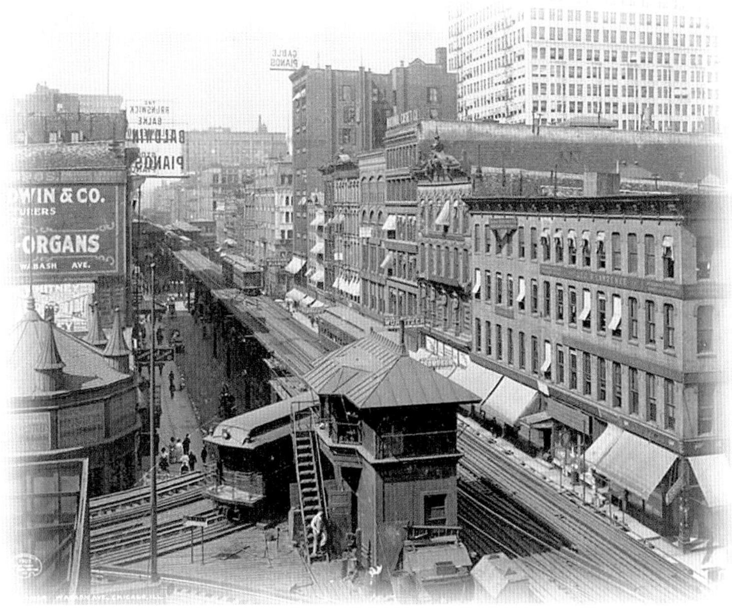

OLD CHICAGO SCENE: Wabash Avenue, c. 1907

Michigan Avenue, Chicago, 1940

THE MICHIGAN AVENUE CLIFF

Stretching from Wacker Drive at the north end to Congress Parkway to the south, the "Michigan Avenue Cliff," also known as the Michigan Boulevard Historic District, is a stretch of road so rich in history and stunning architecture that one could take several different walking tours along the same simple route, seeing different things and taking in different historical sites every time. On

1. Carbide and Carbon Building
2. Smurfit and Stone Building
3. Millennium Park
4. Cloud Gate
5. Crown Fountain
6. Chicago Athletic Association Building
7. Museum of the Art Institute of Chicago
8. Fine Arts Building
9. The Auditorium Theatre
10. Congress Plaza Hotel
11. Grant Park

RIVER NORTH
Merchandise Mart
Chicago River
Michigan
Wacker Dr.
Lake
1
2
AON Center
Randolph
City Hall
Chicago Cultural Center
Millennium Park
3
Prizker Pavilion & Great Lawn
Washington
4
Madison
LOOP
6
5
Monroe
Columbus Dr.
Wacker Dr.
Adams
7
Art Institute of Chicago
The Willis Tower
LaSalle
Jackson
Board of Trade
Van Buren
8
9
Congress PWY
10
Federal
Plymouth Ct.
Harrison
11
Grant Park
Wells
Clark
Dearborn
State
Wabash
Michigan
400m
0.3mile

START:
Carbide and Carbon Building
230 North Michigan Avenue

END:
Grant Park

Tour Time:
About 2 hours

the west side of the street are some of the finest examples of Chicago architecture anywhere, and the east side is lined with fabulous parks and museums. Attempting to point out every site of interest could take an entire book on its own.

We recommend walking on the east side of the street, giving you easy access to the parks and a more panoramic view of the buildings that make up the "Cliff" on the west side.

Carbide and Carbon Building

Elegant lobby details

Smurfit and Stone Building

1. Begin at Wacker Drive and Michigan Avenue, and across the road you will see the unmistakable **Carbide and Carbon Building** at 230 North Michigan Avenue. Now home to the Hard Rock Hotel, the unusual green color makes the building stand out in the skyline; the green facade and gold spire are said to be designed to look like a champagne bottle.

2. Only a block south is the diamond-cutaway **Smurfit and Stone Building** (officially renamed the Crain Communications building in 2012) at 150 North Michigan Avenue, perhaps best known around the country as the building that the main characters repel down in *Adventures in Babysitting*, and as one of the many buildings destroyed in *Transformers: Dark of the Moon*.

3. Proceed one block farther south, and you will find yourself at the entrance to **Millennium Park**, Chicago's newest major tourist attraction. Opening in 2004 with a celebration attended

by some 300,000 people, the park is one of the city's biggest infrastructure projects of the last century. Though work on the park was delayed for years (and set back by the usual trouble with poor planning, accusations of corruption, and other such problems that tend to plague Chicago projects), the end results cannot be denied. Home to the Pritzker Pavilion, an outdoor concert venue, and the icon Crown Fountains, perhaps no part of the park has become more associated with Chicago as "The Bean," the silver bean-like statue officially known as The Cloud Gate.

Millennium Park

Pritzker Pavilion

4. At 100 tons, the gleaming silver **Cloud Gate** is one of the largest pieces of public art in the world. Designed by British artist Anish Kapoor, the mirrored-surface is said to have been inspired by the look of liquid mercury. Kapoor, for his part, hated it when people began to refer to the statue as "The Bean," a description he called "completely stupid," but the name has stuck with the public, and most Chicagoans refer to it that way, not by Kapoor's preferred "Cloud Gate" (he didn't get around to naming the sculpture at all until well after the press had taken to calling it The Bean, by which point it was probably too late). Pause to see your own reflection from underneath, and stand just to the west of it to see a stunning view of The Michigan Avenue Cliff reflected in the surface.

Cloud Gate (a.k.a. "The Bean")

Anish Kapoor

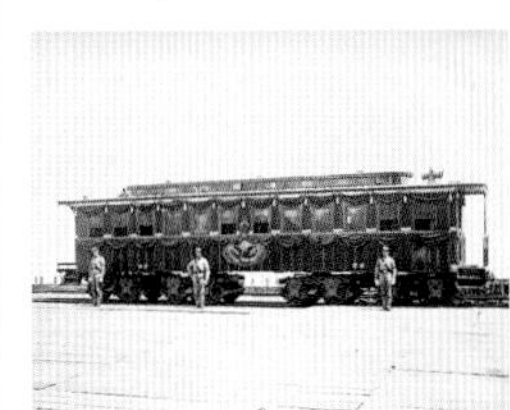
Lincoln's funeral train

One thing to consider as you walk south down Michigan Avenue past The Bean is that you are tracing (in reverse) the path of Abraham Lincoln's funeral carriage. Following Lincoln's assassination, the body was taken "on tour," so that citizens in most major cities had a

Lincoln's funeral, 1865

Crown Fountain

Athletic Association Building

Athletic Association Building, 1907

Interior

chance to pay their respects. Chicago was the last major stop before Springfield, where he was interred. In Chicago, the train carrying his coffin pulled into a station at Michigan Avenue and 12th Street (now Roosevelt Road), and transferred to a carriage that took the remains up Michigan Avenue before turning left into the Loop to the old courthouse, where he was laid in state. At the time, Michigan Avenue was still the lake shore; the only thing east of the street was sand and the lake. The park space was filled in after the Great Chicago Fire of 1871.

5. Just south of Cloud Gate is the **Crown Fountain**, a fountain flanked on the north and south ends by two 50-foot glass towers that function as giant video screens, primarily showing videos of faces of Chicagoans, which change expression from time to time and periodically (in the summer) spit water from their mouths into the fountain space.

6. Proceeding south beyond Millennium Park, look across Michigan Avenue to the west and you will see one of the most gorgeous Venetian Gothic buildings in the world, the **Chicago Athletic Association Building** at 12 South Michigan Avenue. Designed by Henry Ives Cobb to echo the look of the Doge's Palace in Venice, the building (as the name implies), originally housed the Chicago Athletic Association, which used the building as a sort of clubhouse, containing a gym, boxing ring, and beautiful marble swimming pool. Although the building has landmark status, and is protected by law, various proposals have been made to convert the building into a hotel,

and the building is considered "endangered" by preservationists. A preservation-minded firm was chosen to turn it into a boutique hotel, which includes as much of the original interior and details as possible while still breathing new life into the 1893 structure.

7. Proceed another block south and you will find yourself at the unmistakable entrance to the **Museum of the Art Institute of Chicago** at 111 South Michigan Avenue, with the statues of lions that stand guard on either end of the staircase leading towards the Greek Revival museum building (leading many tour guides to crack the joke that people reading on the steps are "reading between the lions").

Museum, Art Institute of Chicago

New wing

Built in 1893 as the World's Congress Building during the World's Fair, the building functioned as a gathering place for "meetings of the minds," including the first conference of leaders of various major religions (which many pinpoint as the introduction of yoga to the United States). Unlike most of the buildings on the main fairgrounds, several miles south down the lake shore, the World's Congress Building was always intended to be permanent; its construction had been advocated by the Art Institute of Chicago, which intended to convert the building into a museum immediately after the fair. The institute moved into the building on Halloween, 1893.

Museum and Grant Park, 1906

During World War I, c. 1917

It is worth stepping aside from the walking tour to see the museum itself, which houses a collection spanning 5,000 years of artwork, containing more than a quarter of a million pieces in all. On display are several works by

Students Making a Mural, 1918

American Gothic (detail), 1930

Grant Wood

Nighthawks (detail), 1942

Edward Hopper

Postcard, c. 1940

such artists as Picasso, Van Gogh, Cezanne, Renoir and Magritte.

Perhaps the two most famous examples of American art in the museum are Grant Wood's *American Gothic*, the classic portrait of the farmer and his wife (or daughter, depending on whom you ask), and Edward Hopper's *Nighthawks*, the timeless portrait of a corner diner in the middle of the night in a big city. *American Gothic* is actually a portrait of Grant Wood's sister and his dentist, and was originally painted by Wood to be entered in a competition held by the Art Institute in 1930. Judges believed the painting to be a sort of "comic Valentine" and a satire of small town life, but they gave it the bronze medal and purchased the painting, little realizing that it would one day be among their biggest draws. Wood was happy to call the painting a satire, but when the Great Depression came and people began to view it as emblematic of the American Midwest's pioneering spirit and old-fashioned values, he was happy to think of it that way, too.

Just as *American Gothic* evokes a mythical sort of view of American small town life, Hopper's 1942 *Nighthawks* is a quintessential view of an American big city at night in the middle of the 20th century. Though thought to be inspired by a now-demolished diner in New York's Greenwich Village, the director of Chicago's Art Institute loved the painting right away, and purchased it for $3,000 within months of its completion, and it has been in the museum's collection ever since.

From the steps, between the lions, you will have a magnificent view of the Gothic-, Baroque- and Art Deco-style buildings that make up the "cliff" across the street. Proceed only a few feet south, and you will be at Michigan Avenue and Jackson Avenue, the beginning of the historic Route 66, which, as the famous song states, "winds from Chicago to L.A." No longer in use as a highway, Route 66 has been portioned off as a series of city streets, access roads and back roads today, though Historic Route 66 points of interest are still visible at several spots along the way.

South from Museum, c.1900-15

8. Proceed another two blocks south down Michigan Avenue, passing Grant Park on the east, across the road to the west will be the Neo-Gothic **Fine Arts Building**, also known as the Studebaker Building, at 410 South Michigan Avenue. Built in 1885 as a display space for Studebaker Carriages, it became a space for fine arts around the turn of the 20th century. Inside, the Art Nouveau-inspired interior includes spaces for theaters, studios, artists' lofts, and offices for such organizations as the Jazz Institute of Chicago. The first floor houses The Artist's Cafe, which has been serving both the resident artists and the public for more than 50 years.

Fine Arts Building

Interior

9. Adjacent to the Fine Arts Building stands **The Auditorium Theatre** (see Chapter 11).

The Auditorium Theatre

Interior of Auditorium Theatre

10. A tunnel beneath Congress Parkway once connected the Auditorium to the **Congress Plaza Hotel** at 520 South Michigan Avenue, which was originally known as the Auditorium Annex. The S wing of the Congress was

Congress Plaza Hotel (left)

Florentine Ballroom

Benny Goodman

Grant Park

Grant Park, 1910

built in 1893, and the interior lobby is still magnificent. Ask a security guard to show you the Florentine Ballroom on the third floor, one of the city's hidden gems. But watch out: like most old hotels, it's said to be haunted. Guests at the hotel over the years included Theodore Roosevelt, Buffalo Bill Cody, Thomas Edison, Franklin Roosevelt, and a long list of 1920s gangsters, many of whom lived in suites in the hotel. Recordings of Benny Goodman and his Orchestra performing in the now-lost Joseph Urban Room for radio broadcasts in the 1930s are available for free online through various sites specializing in archival material; some say that these broadcasts introduced the nation to swing music.

11. Stop in at the lush bar built into the old Elizabethan Room in the hotel for a drink, and take in the magnificent mosaic tiling in the lobby, then cross over Michigan Avenue to enjoy **Grant Park**. Though originally much closer to the Lake Michigan shoreline, the space east of Michigan was designated as park space in 1844. The original plan for the area called for no buildings ever to be built there, but this was ignored for much of the 19th century, and several buildings were erected in the park space at various times (including a baseball stadium that served as an early home for the Chicago Cubs). Renamed for General Ulysses S. Grant in 1901, it was here that Barack Obama held his historic election night rally in 2008.

OLD CHICAGO SCENE: Field Museum of Natural History, c. 1905

Cabaret, South Side Chicago, 1941

INDEX

His New Job, 1915

IMAGE CREDITS

Museyon Guides would like to thank the following organizations and individuals for their guidance and assistance in creating Chronicles of Old Chicago.

Library of Congress
Chicago History Museum
Newberry Library
University of Illinois at Chicago Library
Olga Tymshan
Chicago Postcard Museum

Page 25:
Chicago in 1820, Chicago Lithographing Co., c. 1867, Library of Congress, LC-DIG-pga-03605
Chicago, as it was, between 1856 and 1907, Library of Congress LC-DIG-ppmsca-09545

Page 31:
Uncle Sam's youngest son, Citizen Know Nothing, c. 1854 Library of Congress, LC-DIG-pga-02603

Page 37:
Lincoln's address at the dedication of the Gettysburg National Cemetery, November 19, 1863, Sherwood Lithograph Co., c. 1905, Library of Congress, LC-DIG-ppmsca-19926

Page 39:
An 1850 Campaign banner with Lincoln's first name misspelled, Library of Congress, LC-DIG-pga-01637

Page 42:
Arch at Twelfth St., Chicago, President Abraham Lincoln's hearse and young ladies, S.M. Fassett, 1865, Library of Congress, LC-DIG-ppmsca-19202

Page 43:
Wilkes Booth photographed between 1861 and 1865, Library of Congress, LC-DIG-ppmsca-13706

Page 45:
Abraham Lincoln, candidate for U.S. president, three-quarter length portrait, before delivering his Cooper Union address in New York City, Mathew B. Brady, 1860 February 27, Library of Congress LC-USZ62-5803

Page 47:
In the heart of the Great Union Stock Yards, c. 1909, Library of Congress, LC-USZ62-97324

Page 48:
The Great Union Stock Yards of Chicago, c. 1878, Library of Congress, LC-DIG-pga-02434

Page 51:
Swift & Co.'s Packing House: cutting up hogs, c. 1905, Library of Congress, LC-USZ62-51782

Page 54:
Freight train operations on the Chicago and Northwestern Railroad between Chicago and Clinton, Iowa. Everything is clear and the head brakeman gives engineer the "high ball" or signal to start, Jack Delano, 1943, Library of Congress, LC-USW3-014019-E

Page 57:
The Great Fire at Chicago. Scene, Frank Leslie's illustrated newspaper, 1871 Oct. 28, Library of Congress, LC-USZ62-109590

Page 63:
One of the busiest streets in the world–State St., Chicago, Ill. (18 miles long), N. from Madison St., c. 1903, Library of Congress LC-USZ62-101148

Page 65:
Band concert, Lincoln Park, c. 1907, Library of Congress, LC-D4-70177

Page 66:
Lincoln Memorial, executed by St. Gaudens, Lincoln Park, c. 1908, Library of Congress, LC-USZ62-61673

Page 68:
Shore Drive, Lincoln Park, c. 1905, Library of Congress, LC-D4-18848

Page 69:
Aerial Overview of Lincoln Park along North Lake Shore Drive, after 1969, Library of Congress, HAER ILL, 16-CHIG, 150–1

Page 70:
The Bear pit, Lincoln Park, c. 1901, Library of Congress, LC-D4-12416

Page 73:
Chicago River Bascule Bridge, Michigan Avenue, Spanning Chicago River at North Michigan Avenue, Library of Congress, HAER ILL, 16-CHIG, 129–4

Page 75:
Captain George W. Streeter with wife, sitting in front of their home with their dog, 1915, DN-0064419, Chicago Daily News negatives collection, Chicago History Museum

Page 79:
F.M. Smith & Co., Chicago, Detroit Publishing Co., between 1895 and 1910, Library and Congress, LC-DIG-det-4a20714

Page 81:
Press Correspondents With Lillian Wald And Jane Addams, 1916, Library of Congress, LC-DIG-hec-07331

Page 86:
Peace Delegates on Noordam–Mrs. P. Lawrence, Jane Addams, Anna Molloy, 1915, Library of Congress, LC-DIG-ggbain-18848

Page 94:
Convention crowd at Coliseum, 1912, Library of Congress, LC-DIG-ggbain-10577

Page 96:
Grand banquet given to President Roosevelt at the auditorium by the Iroquois Democratic Club of Chicago, May 10, 1905, Library of Congress, LC-DIG-stereo-1s02150

Page 98:
President Roosevelt's western tour–speaking at Evanston, Illinois, 1903, Library of Congress, c. 1903, LC-DIG- stereo-1s02063

Page 105:
World's Columbian Exposition, Chicago, Ill.: trained animals lined up, with trainers, clowns and others, 1893, Library of

Congress, LC-USZ62-51871

Page 115:
Charles Comiskey, St. Louis Browns, baseball card portrait, 1887, Library of Congress, LC-DIG-bbc-0056f

Page 123:
Mrs. Marie Hermes and Margaret Seithamier sitting on counter in front of bookshelves, 1919, DN-0071130, Chicago Daily News negatives collection, Chicago History Museum

Page 126:
Chicago Criminal Courts Building, 54 West Hubbard Street, 1964, Library of Congress, HABS ILL,16-CHIG,38–1

Page 131:
A woman dressed in flapper fashion delivers a speech from a soapbox, Newberry Library

Page 157:
Billy Goat Tavern, Chicago sports fan's landmark, Chicago, between 1980 and 2006, Library of Congress, LC-DIG-highsm-12253

Page 172:
Newberry Library, Chicago, Library of Congress, LC-DIG-det-4a08709

Page 187:
Richard J. Daley views skyline in 1966 from atop then-new Daley Center, UIC Library Special Collections

Page 188:
Richard J. Daley and Queen Elizabeth II during her 1959 visit to Chicago, UIC Library Special Collections

Page 191:
The Fresh Prince Of Bel-Air, (from left): Oprah Winfrey, Will Smith, 'A Night At The Oprah', (Season 3, aired Nov. 9, 1992), 1990-96. © NBC / Courtesy: Everett Collection, TBDFRPR EC017

Page 197:
Union Station concourse, Jack Delano, 1943, Library of Congress, LC-USW3-015485-E

Page 199:
Barack Obama at a public appearance for Barack Obama U.S. Presidential Election Victory Speech and Celebration, Grant Park, Chicago, IL, November 04, 2008. Photo by: Kristin Callahan/Everett Collection, 0804NVC KH031

Page 206:
Dearborn Street station, between 1910 and 20, Library of Congress, LC-DIG-det-4a24000

Page 214:
Chicago River east from Rush St. Bridge, c. 1905, Library of Congress, LC-DIG-det-4a12889

Page 224:
In front of the movie theater. Chicago, Russel Lee, 1941, Library of Congress, LC-USF34-038814-D

Page 231:
Seeing Chicago, auto at Monroe near State, Detroit Publishing Co., between 1900 and 1915, Library of Congress, LC-DIG-det-4a19702

Page 232:
Around a bubbling cup, Lincoln Park, Chicago, between 1910 and 20, Library of Congress, LC-DIG-det-4a24796

Page 240:
The Heart of Chicago, c. 1900 or 1901, Library of Congress, LC-DIG-det-4a07949

Page 249:
Wabash Ave., Chicago, Detroit Publishing Co., c. 1907, Library of Congress, LC-USZ62-116114

Page 250:
Michigan Avenue, Chicago, John Vachon, 1940, Library of Congress, LC-USF33-001914-M1

Page 259:
Field Museum (of Natural History), Chicago, Detroit Publishing Co., c. 1905, Library of Congress, LC-DIG-det-4a12884

Page 260:
Cabaret. Chicago, Russel Lee, 1941, Library of Congress, LC-DIG-fsa-8c00639

Page 218-4: Marina City, Page 220-1: Clark Street Bridge, Page 222-4: LaSalle Street Bridge, Page 223-4: View from the Mart, Page 246-4, 5: Willis Tower, Page 247-2, 3: View from the Willis Tower, © Olga Tymshan

Page 235-2: Couch Family Mausoleum, Page 239-1:
Site of Valentine's Day massacre, © Adam Selzer

Page 255-4, 5: Art Institute of Chicago, Courtesy of Chicago Postcard Museum, www.ChicagoPostcardMuseum.org

Page 270:
Adam Selzer, © Jen Hathy

ABOUT MUSEYON

Named after the Museion, the ancient Egyptian institute dedicated to the muses, Museyon Guides is an independent publisher that explores the world through the lens of cultural obsessions. Intended for frequent fliers and armchair travelers alike, our books are expert-curated and carefully researched, offering rich visuals, practical tips and quality information.

MUSEYON'S OTHER TITLES

Film + Travel Europe 9780982232002
Film + Travel Asia, Oceania, Africa 9780982232019
FIlm + Travel North America, South America 9780982232026
Music + Travel Worldwide 9780982232033
Art + Travel Europe 9780982232057
Chronicles of Old New York 9780982232064
City Style 9780982232071
Art + NYC 9780982232088
Art + Paris: Impressionists and Post-Impressionists 9780982232095
Chronicles of Old Las Vegas 9780984633418
Chronicles of Old Paris 9780984633425
Chronicles of Old Boston 9780984633401
Chronicles of Old London 9780984633432
Chronicles of Old Rome 9780984633449
On Location NYC 9780984633463
Cool Japan 9780984633456
The Golden Moments of Paris 9780984633470

Pick one up and follow your interests...wherever they might go.
For more information vist www.museyon.com. www.facebook.com/museyon and www.twitter.com/museyon. Inquiries: info@museyon.com

Museyon Inc.

Publisher: Akira Chiba
Editor: Janice Battiste
Assistant Editor: Mackenzie Allison
Cover Design: José Antonio Contreras
Design & Layout: West 61 Company
SN Marketing: Sara Marquez

ABOUT THE AUTHOR

Adam Selzer, a historian and tour guide, was born in Des Moines and makes his home in Chicago, where he resides with his wife, stepson and cats in the west Loop. The passionate Chicago-lover appears regularly on TV and radio talking about Chicago history, and he has published 15 books, ranging from young adult novels to books on the history of the Windy City including the recent *Ghosts of Chicago*. He can often be found writing in coffee shops or poking around old buildings, empty alleyways, and dusty libraries around the city.